Public Speaking

Is A Skill,

Not A Talent

The 7 Stages of Effective Communication

DEBORAH ROFFEY

To anyone wishing to overcome
their fear of Public Speaking and
is willing to face their demon,
this is dedicated to you.

Children's Books by the same author:

Trouble With Boys Series:

       Billy's Bubble – Book 1

       See you Slater – Book 2

       Forget Me Not – Book 3

My Life series:

       My Life In Darkness

Picture Books:

       At The Airshow

More to come …

Author's websites:

       www.deborahroffey.com

       www.premierpublicspeaking.com.au

An effective speech is like a priceless liqueur,
and the audience's attention the glass – pour
every word into it, as if it were the last drop.

This page is intentionally left blank.

Contents

This page is intentionally left blank.

PREFACE

Dallas Brooks Hall, 1993

I will never forget the first time I spoke in front of an audience: It was a massive stage and I felt so small; my voice was quavering, hands shaking, palms sweating, and knees like jelly, about to buckle. I was terrified... and in the audience were around three thousand of my peers, witnessing every ghastly moment!

It wasn't the content that let me down, at least not that I could recall – I had a message to deliver and I believe I did that, judging by the response I received. Following the event, as I rode the elevator heading back to my office, a few of my colleagues, some I'd never met before, commended me on my speech.

One comment, in particular, stood out: "You made some terrific points and were very passionate," he said.

Then it came ... "Were you crying?" he asked.

In fifteen seconds, I'd gone from receiving a congratulatory slap on the back, to what resembled a slap across the face! On stage, I had been scared and my voice shaky, yet I was sure I'd gotten away with it. Who was I fooling? It had not gone unnoticed. I was mortified!

It's odd, really, as he probably never gave it another thought. But I couldn't get it out of my mind. I returned to my office and sat at my desk, struggling futilely to concentrate on my work, but I couldn't shake my embarrassment and humiliation at his comment. I mulled it over for several hours, trying to brush it off, or seeking excuses for myself, each time reaching the same conclusion: I can never let it happen again. I want to improve my self-confidence and, to do that, I need to learn how to speak publicly, properly, and confidently.

Time wore on and life got in the way, as it so often does, and it was not until many years later that I finally took the first step toward personal and professional development and public speaking training. Only then did I realise I was not alone. As I delved further into it, I became acutely aware of the widespread fear of public speaking. Each person I spoke to experienced real anxiety - physical and mental - when called upon to speak publicly. It can happen in any situation, at any given time. I was surprised to learn even professional speakers suffered prior to, or whilst, performing. I witnessed brave peers seeking help to face their demons and conquer their fear.

I studied, practised, and delivered countless speeches and presentations for more than two decades. As a result, I was continually approached to coach or mentor speakers and would-be speakers who, for various reasons – personal or professional – were required to speak publicly.

Several years on, I became a qualified trainer and launched my business, Premier Public Speaking, coaching other sufferers, helping them to conquer their fear, build their confidence, and learn simple delivery techniques, to be the confident speakers they want to be.

A single, precipitous, albeit innocent comment, was to change my life and eventually lead to this book.

INTRODUCTION

"How on earth do you get up on stage and speak in front of all these people?" I am frequently asked this question and the answer is simple: I learned how to conquer my fear and speak with confidence and clarity.

Communication and interpersonal skills are paramount for everyone, whether it's in everyday life or as essential skills of a good leader. In reality, the two go hand-in-hand, but many people struggle to develop these skills due to a lack of confidence and proper training.

The adage, 'a fear of public speaking is considered the number one fear' is not quite true … but it comes close. It is one of the most common fears. Even social situations can cause severe anxiety and panic for some, let alone speaking in front of a larger audience!

Imagine throwing away that fear, walking to the lectern, head held high, and confidently launching into your speech! Does that sound like you? Or is it something you strive for and yearn to do? Whether for professional or personal reasons, this book is dedicated to helping you achieve that goal.

Skill: *Noun* - ability to do something well, having learned & practised.

Talent: *Noun* - natural aptitude or ability to be good at something.

Public Speaking is not a talent you're born with, it's a skill learned over time and, with practice, one that most people can achieve. Speakers use both visual and auditory communication to articulate their message to an audience. Accomplished speakers put hundreds, sometimes thousands, of hours into learning, preparing, and executing delivery techniques, honing their skills until they are satisfied that they have achieved the level of competency needed for their profession.

Referring to a speaker as an accomplished speaker doesn't mean they are a professional speaker. It means that, no matter what career or position they are in – teacher, salesman, customer service operator, team member, manager, facilitator, or professional speaker – they are proficient, having gained the confidence and skills required to communicate effectively and engage their audience.

Public speaking is not just an art, it is a science, too. There are a range of techniques we can use to be an effective communicator, ensuring our audience is engaged and the message listened to, understood, and absorbed. We want the audience to hear what we're saying, understand what we're talking about, relate to our story, and leave with whatever important message we are trying to convey.

In this book, I explain the fundamental techniques for effective communication, providing practical, tried, and tested methods to improve your confidence and public speaking skills. The techniques are easy to practise and achieve, to help you become a better speaker, and simple enough to incorporate in your personal and professional life, enabling you to communicate effectively and with confidence.

Are you ready to take the first step toward conquering your fear? Then read on …

CHAPTER 1

The First Step

You Are Not Alone

Communication is the lifeblood of understanding;
confidence is the key to success;
authenticity is the path to take you there.

Communication is a massive part of our everyday lives. We use communication in our speech, body language, writing, and digital technology, to express ourselves and convey our message to others. Whatever we communicate, from the simplest comment to innovative ideas and complex solutions, we need to convey our message authentically and effectively, to be successful in our personal and professional lives.

It's all well-and-good knowing this, but how do we execute it in a way that leaves us feeling fulfilled and having achieved what we set out to do, when all we really want to do is hide in a corner, somewhere, especially if called upon to speak impromptu - on the spur of the moment? The horror of it all! "Ask someone else!"

When we see someone speak in front of an audience, for example, delivering a speech, acting in a play on stage, or a colleague reporting on a team's progress at work, we're often in awe and envy:

"I wish I could do that." "She is so confident." "That was terrific!"

Audience feedback, such as this, is typical of many who fear public speaking, themselves. If we ask these same people to speak in front of an audience, their responses are generally, "No way!" or "I can't."

When I inquire with my clients why they want to be coached, their responses are surprisingly similar, often including some or all of the following: "When I'm asked to speak at work, I'm terrified. I find myself shaking and I can't think straight, my voice quivers, and I'm sweating. I forget everything I'm supposed to say and sound like I'm burbling. I want to be able to speak confidently and clearly."

It is the same around the world. You are not alone.

You don't have to be a professional speaker to want to speak confidently and clearly, either. It could be one or more of literally thousands of reasons you might need these skills: as Best Man at your friend's wedding to prepare and deliver a speech for the reception; as a student, participating in debating, or delivering a project to the class; at work, reporting on the progress or project outcomes at team meetings; when preparing for upcoming job interviews; as a manager, your interpersonal skills need refinement; you find it difficult to respond to questions clearly and succinctly; in social situations, you struggle to interact. These are just a few of many situations which can find us anxious, tongue-tied, speechless, and terrified and, perhaps, ducking for cover!

The key to success is conquering our fear, practising the skills we need to speak with confidence, and being ourselves. As practised, skilled, authentic public speakers, we will have the edge over other, less skilled communicators, empowering us to communicate effectively with our audience. We must learn to control the anxiety and use it to our advantage.

Fear Factor

Fear often stops us before we begin. Fear of failure,
of being judged, of the unknown. Life begins when
we take the first step out of our comfort zone.

Our fears are not baseless – there is clear evidence that Glossophobia, the fancy term used for the fear of public speaking, is real. For some, it is debilitating, but it can have devastating effects even for mild sufferers.

Many people suffer a lack of confidence – it is at the core of their fear of public speaking. Performance pressure, too, can be overwhelming, as can the fear of humiliation or failure, of making mistakes, forgetting lines, or inexperience. However, lack of preparation is, usually, a major contributing factor, which we will discuss in more detail in other chapters.

A negative public speaking experience can have lifelong consequences, as our natural protective instincts kick into gear, preventing us from taking up future opportunities; career or business prospects suddenly cease and our self-confidence plunges deeper into the void.

Self-doubt and insecurity can control us, if left unchecked, limiting our capacity to succeed in our personal and professional lives. But it doesn't have to always be that way.

We need to ask ourselves, "Am I prepared to take the first step toward self-improvement?" and "Am I truly committed to achieving my goal?" If the answer is yes, there are simple techniques we can learn and practise regularly to build our confidence and work toward overcoming, or controlling, our anxiety.

First, we need to identify and understand what are the driving forces, the main factors, that create this, at times, crippling fear? Several factors contribute to fear. The more we comprehend and recognize the contributing factors that cause our apprehension, the more likely we are to be able to manage and overcome them. There are four main factors involved.

Physiology

Noun - the way in which a living organism or bodily part functions.

How we think, feel, or act is reflected in our emotional state which, in turn, generates physical changes to our bodies, some of which are subtle, whilst others are quite conspicuous. A lack of confidence causes a person to feel anxious, triggering a physiological response.

As we are confronted with a potential threat, whether real or perceived, the nervous system stimulates our body to prepare it for battle. Adrenalin, noradrenaline, and cortisol are released into the bloodstream, placing our bodies on high alert. This produces the emotional response of fear – our survival mechanism. The fight-or-flight response is an automatic and instinctive response to fear, bypassing the rational or conscious mind.

Sufferers may experience one or many symptoms, depending on their physiological response. Such physiological responses are 'normal' and we can learn strategies to manage and, in many cases, overcome them.

The most common of these, some of which are less obvious to an audience, include:

- Increased heart rate
- Excessive sweating
- Dry mouth
- Shaking
- Voice quavering
- Butterflies in the stomach
- Rapid, shallow breathing

- Excessive change in body temperature

- Recurring negative thoughts

- Upset stomach/Diarrhea

Symptoms do not discriminate - they can affect anyone, from novices to practised and accomplished speakers, with varying degrees of intensity and discomfort, from slight to extreme. This physical discomfort can also cause any number of more obvious responses, such as: speaking rapidly, or not at all; avoiding eye contact with the audience and seeking the script on the ceiling or floor; uttering filler or linking words, rather than pauses; fidgeting with our hands or clothing.

On the other hand, viewed positively, the heightened state of readiness anxiety puts you in can increase energy levels and help you speak better.

Fear of public speaking symptoms are many and varied and tend to peak at the beginning of speaking to audiences. However, they can last the entirety of the speech, if not managed effectively.

Mindset

Noun - a person's way of thinking; the established set of attitudes held by someone.

The sooner you activate improvement,
the sooner you deactivate self-criticism.

It is important to remember that public speaking will not likely kill you! It may feel like the end of the world whilst on stage, but you will recover - once off stage your heart rate and breathing will return to normal and you will realise you survived. Hooray!

I do not mean to sound belittling in any way. We know the fear is real – I can speak from personal experience - which reinforces why it is so important to work toward managing and overcoming it, so you feel comfortable and confident speaking publicly. It is important to understand that most of what you feel is internal - the audience is usually totally unaware of what you are experiencing – the audience can't see it.

How we perceive ourselves and situations has a massive impact on how we conduct ourselves and react. Many people have an unhealthy opinion of themselves. This, of course, is closely linked to their level of confidence and this mindset frequently creates a barrier to success. Those on the lower confidence spectrum often have a fear of failure, an unrealistic expectation of what a good speaker is, believe they have nothing worthy or interesting to contribute, or a combination of these things. Such thoughts are obstructive to growth, preventing us from taking up public speaking opportunities.

"I'll probably get booed off the stage."
"What if I forget what I'm supposed to say?"
"I'll look like a fool. They'll hate me."

The fear of failure often arises when we overestimate the stakes involved and the expectations of the audience, overly concerning ourselves with the prospect of receiving a negative audience reaction, potential loss of credibility or image, and anxiety of feeling judged.

"I could never be that good."
"I'm too old to learn to speak that well."

An unrealistic expectation of what a good speaker is can intimidate and scare us off, too. People tend to believe good speakers are perfect, fearless, experts in their field, and have a right to be there – considering them far superior to themselves.

Placing speakers on a pedestal is impractical. Many have suffered similar experiences to you at some stage in their lives, too. They have suffered anxiety and dread, nervousness, shaking, dry mouth; they have made mistakes, forgotten sections of their speech, and fumbled for words. In reality, they are just ordinary people who learned how to improve their confidence, utilise simple delivery techniques, and embrace an important phrase – 'practice, practice, practice'.

"I'm boring, no-one will be interested in hearing me speak."
"Everyone is better than me."
"My ideas aren't important."

I am constantly amazed by the number of people who unjustly believe they have nothing interesting to say, or worthwhile listening to and, therefore, avoid speaking in many situations, even in informal or social gatherings.

So much goes unsaid. Instead of actively participating in conversation, or proffering an idea or solution, they sit quietly, saying nothing, either believing they'll just be wasting people's time with uninteresting guff, or are afraid of appearing foolish.

What they fail to understand is, people can be deeply affected by the sharing of inspirational stories and ideas, important work, and effectual solutions. It makes us wonder, how much have we missed out on? The answer is immeasurable, of course. Sadly, it is our loss.

It is paramount that we alter the mindset of those suffering from a fear of public speaking and encourage them to build their confidence and conquer their fear. I hope this book will assist to affect change.

Condition

Noun - the circumstances or factors affecting the way in which people live or work, especially with regard to their well-being.

The condition or situation we are presented with affects our level of fear and anxiety. Each condition can hamper our ability to perform in public.

It may be the first time you've ever spoken in front of an audience, or you have very little experience and not yet developed the confidence that practice creates.

You may have been longing to share an idea or story for some time and are suddenly confronted with the thought that maybe your audience won't share your enthusiasm or will ask difficult questions, putting you on the spot. Perhaps the familiar environment of your team is suddenly changed when your boss asks you to pitch your idea to senior management or an important client.

Such conditions can produce mild to severe levels of anxiety, fuelling our fear.

Expertise

Noun - expert skill or knowledge in a particular field.

Public Speaking is a skill, not a talent. We are not born to be speakers. It is true some people appear to have a natural ability to speak publicly, but this natural ability is generally coupled with countless hours of preparation – planning, writing, learning, practising, and gaining experience.

Increased exposure leads to greater expertise which, in turn, leads to an increase in confidence.

Believing that you need to be an expert in public speaking before you are capable of having a go, is a paradox – it is not possible to become an effective communicator without practice, and you cannot practise until you have a go!

No speaker is perfect. Some of the most influential speakers in the world have made mistakes, such as forgotten a line or two, tripped on stage, or dropped a prop. And guess what? They survived! At some stage, we will make mistakes, too. Throughout this book, you will learn techniques to deal with these issues, so they don't leave you feeling that your world is falling apart.

You do not need to be an astrophysicist to talk about the stars, nor a brain surgeon to speak about suffering a stroke. There is still a potential speech up everyone's sleeve, based on knowledge, life experience, and interests.

You may know little about a particular topic or subject, but what you do know might still be worth sharing. Your speech may contain a crucial piece of information missing from a puzzle, have the answer to someone's question, or simply be a really interesting story – you'll never know if it's never delivered.

We have identified and, hopefully, now understand, the four contributing factors that can cripple us with fear:

Physiology: our body's natural reaction to fear,

Mindset: the impact of negative thoughts & perceptions,

Condition: situations we may be confronted with, and

Expertise: the effects of lack of practice and inexperience.

Now let's focus on managing them.

CHAPTER 2
Taking Action

Preparing for Battle

*We cannot reach our goal without taking
the first step to begin our journey.*

Congratulations! If you are continuing to read this book, you
have taken the next step on your journey to conquering your
fear of public speaking. Now comes the practical part to facing
your demons, so prepare yourself for battle.

A little melodramatic perhaps because, in fact, the battle will
only be with yourself, as everyone around you will likely be
encouraging and supporting you every step of the way.

Many clients ask me, "Where do I start?" or "What is the best
way to attack my problem?"

The most effective method is, undoubtedly, exposure –
confronting the problem head-on and immersing yourself in
the situation – but this is a dramatic and challenging scenario

for many and can have the opposite effect, if not properly prepared, and may put you off from ever trying again.

The aim is to prepare you first. Once you have learned to manage your anxiety and practised the techniques for effective communication, your confidence will have improved, you will be equipped with the necessary skills, and ready to deliver your speech in front of an audience. It's unlikely to be your best performance, but it will certainly be a better, more pleasurable experience for you and one which you can build on.

There are several ways to take the first step on your learning journey:

- Private coaching is, of course, ideal and the preferred method of learning – it is invaluable. Tailored lessons focus on your individual needs and goals, and aid in fast-tracking your journey, whilst providing immediate, expert feedback from a trained professional, which is then incorporated into future tasks/speeches.

  You will benefit from practising in front of your coach, so you can work on areas that require improvement before delivering in front of an audience.

  Your coach may assist you with organising speaking engagements to practise in front of an audience, as well as utilising technology, such as audio-visual equipment, correct procedure when working with a microphone, and the recording of sessions to evaluate your progress.

- Joining a public speaking group, such as Toastmasters or Rostrum, will certainly provide opportunities to speak in front of an audience, as well as receive feedback, albeit from untrained fellow members. Speaking slots are limited, however, so the pace of learning can be slow and irregular. Consider joining one of these groups in conjunction with private coaching.

- Enrolling in a public speaking workshop, run by a qualified professional, is a good compromise between private coaching and joining a public speaking group, especially when finances are stretched. Workshops generally focus on specific areas to develop and hone, rather than an individual's needs, and offer more opportunities to speak in front of audiences (depending on the number of participants), to gain experience. Workshop facilitators should provide feedback to participants throughout the course, enabling them to incorporate suggested improvements into future tasks/speeches.

- Choosing to tackle this problem alone will probably take much longer, especially as there is little chance, if any, for practice and no chance of receiving any objective feedback, before delivering your speech to an audience. If you are considering working alone, do so temporarily, then continue in conjunction with private coaching, to achieve better results, faster.

Once you have decided on a learning approach, the next step is to actually do it! Unless you are truly committed, you are unlikely to succeed.

Over the years, I have observed numerous clients signing up to various speaking groups or courses, only to discover they are too scared to step through the door and have wasted the money they invested. Often, they feel overwhelmed, intimidated, or too shy learning in a group environment, preferring to enrol in private coaching. Some lose heart at the slow pace of improvement and their commitment level wanes.

Clients enrol in private coaching, where they feel comfortable, supported, and in a non-threatening environment. The simple fact they didn't give up and, instead, sought private coaching, is evidence of their commitment to improving themselves and they should be applauded. Many gain enough confidence to later branch into workshops, intensive coaching courses, and public speaking groups, which helps to ease any financial strain.

Private Coaching is suitable for speakers of all levels, from beginner to accomplished professional. There is much to learn, practise, and hone - we can never be perfect or know too much!

Relieving Anxiety

You may experience fear and anxiety from public speaking, or the mere thought of speaking in public, regardless of the amount of preparation you have done, but you are not unique.

Make no mistake, your fear is very real, but it *is* manageable. Actors, professional speakers, presenters, teachers, and more have all experienced fear in some form and most continue to experience it throughout their careers, but have found ways to manage the fear.

Each person suffers varying degrees of anxiety and fear of public speaking when thinking about, preparing for, and presenting in front of an audience. The symptoms can be combated with a range of relaxation techniques to put our body in a calm state. It is advisable to practise each of the different techniques to determine which are most effective for you and use a combination of the best techniques to achieve greater results.

Breathing

Breathlessness on stage is common. Poor, shallow, or rapid breathing creates an oxygen deficiency, making the heart's ability to pump blood out less efficient. This leads to bad circulation, and cold hands and feet, together with tightening and stiffness of muscles. If your shoulders rise and fall as you breathe, less oxygen is getting to your heart.

Learning to control your breathing assists in lowering your heart rate, which in turn lessens the tension in your muscles. You can do this by changing your breathing habits through diaphragmatic breathing. Breathing in through your nose, rather than your mouth, is a healthy habit to get into, as it filters the air on intake and is more likely to reach your diaphragm. Diaphragmatic breathing can be practised at home, at work, on the train, waiting to go on stage … in fact, almost anywhere!

Here are 7 easy steps to practising diaphragmatic breathing:

1. Lie on your back on a flat surface or bed, with your knees bent and head supported. Use a pillow or rolled towel under your knees for support. If impractical, find a comfortable chair to sit in.

2. Place one hand on your upper chest, the other on your belly.

3. Close your mouth. Breathe in through your nose, slowly and

deeply. You should feel your belly expand against your hand. The hand on your chest should remain as still as possible.

4. Hold for 2 seconds

5. Exhale through your mouth, pursing your lips as you do so. Your lower hand should fall inward gently as your belly contracts. Again, the hand on your chest should remain as still as possible.

6. Hold for 2 seconds

7. Repeat steps 3 to 6 for around 3-5 minutes (longer, if anxiety levels are high)

Nose Inhale → Hold 2" → Mouth Exhale → Hold 2"

This exercise can be quite tiring at first, but the more you practise, the easier it will become and, eventually, will become automatic.

As you perfect the diaphragmatic breathing technique, try extending your inhale, exhale, and hold times by 1 or 2 seconds, such as inhale and hold for 3 seconds, exhale and hold for 3-4 seconds, and repeat.

Try this:

Nose Inhale → Hold 3" → Mouth Exhale → Hold 3"

Practise breathing this way as often as you can to relieve anxiety and tension. It is an excellent technique, particularly when combined with meditation.

Meditation

Simple meditation techniques can be used to cope with the stress and anxiety that your body and mind experiences dealing with fear. Short-term effects include lower blood pressure, improved blood circulation, lower heart rate, and less stress and anxiety, resulting in a feeling of well-being.

If you have never meditated before, there are literally thousands of meditation recordings available, ranging from calming music to a soothing voice talking you through mindfulness relaxation exercises. They will assist you to meditate, putting you into the calm, serene state that you want to feel, whilst helping to control your breathing.

Relaxation meditation is an effective technique, offering quick results, but won't necessarily have long-lasting effects. Incorporating meditation whilst practising diaphragmatic breathing is much more effective and can take relaxation to the next level. It will help you to redirect your focus more easily, concentrating on yourself, rather than your fear.

Follow the diaphragmatic breathing technique, practising until you are confident you can do it properly. Then try adding this simple meditation exercise to your routine:

1. Find a quiet place away from distractions. You may choose to have some soothing instrumental music playing quietly in the background.

2. Close your eyes, whilst performing the diaphragmatic breathing technique.

3. Focus solely on your breathing – the inhalation and exhalation of each breath, feeling your hand resting on your belly as it rises and falls.

   If your mind wanders, be mindful of the random thoughts, but let them go and refocus on your breathing. The intention is not to get involved with or judge the thoughts, just be aware of them. With practice, your ability to concentrate more on your breathing and less on your thoughts will improve, as will the time required to achieve effectiveness.

4. Meditate for as long as needed and time permits.

If you are experiencing difficulty meditating, you may wish to use a meditation recording to guide you through the process. You may also wish to try thinking of a situation or place in which you feel completely at peace or concentrate on the soothing instrumental music playing in the background. Allow all your thoughts to focus on the peace and serenity that the situation, place, or music makes you feel.

Exposure

"Procrastination is the thief of time."
Charles Dickens

It is human nature to delay or avoid things we dislike and, for most people, the hardest thing to contend with is confronting their fear. Many people play the avoidance game, seeking any excuse or alternative to facing it head-on, thereby never overcoming the problem.

Whether your fear begins at the mere thought of public speaking, preparing to speak, or actually presenting in front of an audience, putting it off, avoiding, or refusing to confront the problem, will result in failing to overcome it and a continual cycle of anxiety and fear.

Instead, we need to channel our nervous energy and turn it into positive energy, enabling our audience to view our heightened state as excitement or enthusiasm.

Pairing the previous two fear-management techniques with gradual exposure to public speaking is the ideal way to manage anxiety.

Employ the techniques when you first agree to speak, then again, as you prepare your speech, and continue to apply them when you eventually present it. Picture yourself delivering the speech, from beginning to end, concluding with rousing applause from the audience. Visualising your success will help to grow self-confidence, rather than focusing on your fear.

Accept and seek out opportunities to speak publicly, to gain exposure and practice. Start with very small audiences, gradually increasing numbers as your confidence improves. This could be with friends, colleagues, or community groups and the like. As you learn how to successfully manage your anxiety through relaxation, you could begin steadily increasing the scale of the events.

Consider starting with speeches that are easier to prepare and less scary to deliver. This will help as you master the relaxation techniques. Slowly but surely, introduce speaking opportunities where the stakes are increasingly higher. Don't rush in – you will know when you are ready.

Preparation

"By failing to prepare, you are preparing to fail."
Benjamin Franklin

This is an extremely important subject, which cannot be emphasised enough. We will touch on it here, but discuss it in greater detail later in the book.

Getting up and speaking in front of an audience can be nerve-wracking. Couple this with an ill-prepared speech or a poorly practised presenter, and you have the perfect recipe for disaster. But how can we prevent a disaster from occurring in the first place?

There are three important 'Ps' of a successful *speaker.*

Preparation, Preparation, Preparation.

We are all guilty of making excuses for not getting things done: we didn't have enough time, couldn't think of something to write about, had too much else on, and so forth. However, they are just that – excuses.

Generally, most people believe the biggest problem they face is their fear. However, that fear is exacerbated by a lack of preparation.

Many speakers procrastinate, leaving things till the last minute, allowing little or no time to prepare a speech, or maybe even 'winging it,' and are left wondering why they are so nervous, perform poorly, and are poorly received.

Whether it's planning, writing, editing, or practising your speech, it cannot be stressed enough the importance of prioritising your time to allow plenty of preparation. And it is pointless preparing the perfect speech to deliver if you fail to prepare yourself. You are truly doing yourself and your audience a disservice if you do not prepare well.

Preparation will naturally help to increase your confidence, which will relieve much of the fear you would otherwise endure. The breathing exercises, meditation, and exposure techniques should also become part of your routine if you find they are working for you.

Always remember, your degree of commitment to preparation will either make or break your speech, so don't let yourself or your audience down.

CHAPTER 3

An Effective Speech

"… I was a mayor, and they're probably thinking I know how to give speeches, but even when I was mayor, I never gave speeches. I gave talks."
Clint Eastwood

For every speech, it is paramount to understand the topic, level of detail and formality suitable for its audience, and desired result, to effectively communicate your message or information. But what does that mean? Consider:

1. **What** do you want to communicate to the listener;

2. **How** should you interpret the message to each audience;

3. **What** action should the listener take following the speech?

For example, a speech on reducing waste products in landfill might consist of:

1. **What** – highlighting the need to reduce landfill;

2. **How** – using facts and anecdotes to support the idea and make the audience aware of the serious landfill issue;

3. **What** – audience to make a conscious effort to recycle waste products to reduce landfill, wherever possible.

Once these three important factors are determined, there are many more questions you must ask yourself, before preparing a speech:

- Who is the audience;

- Why this message to this audience;

- Why now;

- What content to include;

- How to structure the speech;

- What language is appropriate;

- What props or aids to use, if any;

- What technique and delivery style to use?

These questions and more are at the heart of creating an effective speech and we will address them in this chapter. Merely focussing on a single or several aspects, without considering the whole picture, will result in a less effective and engaging speech. And every speech you deliver will be different, depending on its audience.

Speech Style

Several factors play a role in determining how we express ourselves to others. Whilst each person has their unique style of verbal interaction, the style of communication changes, according to social, situational, environmental, and societal expectation. Therefore, how you tell a story one day, might be completely different from the next.

Articulating a message to another person or persons requires careful consideration about how we want it to be told. For instance, when talking with a loved one or friend, we might speak conversationally or casually with them. Conversely, a similar conversation held be in a more formal setting would likely require the language and style to be completely different.

Each time we speak spontaneously, we choose, albeit sometimes unconsciously, a speech style to convey our message. When delivering a speech, we must use a more planned approach. Careful consideration and selection of an appropriate style for specific events helps prevent conflicts or misunderstanding by the listener.

According to a study by linguist and German professor, Martin Joos (1976:156), speech style means "the form of language that the speaker uses which characterized by the degree of formality."[1] This refers to the distinctive way of communication.

In his study, Joos identified five main language registers based on formality, more commonly known as speech styles. They are frozen, formal, consultative, casual, and intimate.

Here we examine speech styles, individually:

1. **Frozen** – also known as **fixed speech**, it is the most formal communicative style, which is often used in formal ceremonies and other respectful events; usually delivered oratorically, it uses complex grammatical sentence structure and vocabulary, and does not require any feedback, nor accept questions, from the audience.

   Examples: Pledges, weddings, funerals, laws, bible quotations.

2. **Formal** – used at formal events and occasions, and prepared in advance, this one-way communicative style uses precise definitions, complex sentences & phrases, which are well structured & articulate, and avoids the use of slang terminology, abbreviations, or contractions; audience interaction is neither invited nor expected.

   Examples: Announcements, opening ceremonies, reports, official documents, textbooks.

3. **Consultative** – commonly used between strangers, or persons who are neither friends nor family, this semi-formal, often unplanned, or spontaneous, two-way communication style, uses shorter sentencing structure, and requires or invites participation from the audience; background information is provided and the listener participates continuously; a highly interactive communicative style between speaker and listener.

   Examples: Classroom discussions, job interviews, Lawyer-client.

4. **Casual** – this is an informal communicative style, usually between groups of friends or colleagues, who share common ground, but not a close relationship; uses shorter sentences & phrases, slang, and colloquialisms; a relaxed, free & easy two-way participation between speaker and listener.

   Examples: Conversation among friends, phone calls, emails, chats.

5. **Intimate** – a very relaxed, informal communicative style between people who are extremely close and share a common bond; nonverbal communication features prominently, words are used sparingly; a relaxed, free & easy two-way participation between speaker and listener.

   Examples: Husband & wife, best friends, family discussions.

Joos also acknowledged that it is possible to shift between styles whilst speaking, though speakers generally tended to only shift to more than one level in jest.

Whatever way you deliver your speech or conversation, it should always be audience-centred and appear natural and authentic.

The Building Blocks

"The difference between something good and
something great is the attention to detail."
Charles R. Swindoll

If you have jumped ahead to this section, most likely you are a confident person, who feels able to stand in front of an audience of any size and demographic. That's fabulous! Many speakers aspire to reach that level of confidence, so we applaud you.

If you have worked your way gradually to this section, well done – your concerted effort is to be commended. Confidence is an important life-skill to acquire. It is the cornerstone of a successful public speaker. And by now, you understand that to deliver an effective speech, there is so much more involved than first thought.

Every speaker wants to be respected by their audience. They want the audience to listen attentively; proactively engage when asked; understand the purpose of their message, that is, leave knowing more than they did before, or agree with, or act on, the speaker's message; and provide feedback to the speaker, such as showing interest in the topic with follow up questions and applause.

Likewise, every speech and every audience should be treated with respect. After all, your audience doesn't have to be there. Rather than present you with an empty room or auditorium, they have chosen to come along, and perhaps paid, to listen and see you deliver your speech – they deserve your best effort. Whether it's a brief response to a question or a lengthy keynote address, always make it an effective speech.

An effective speech is like a tower: it can be broken down into elements, or building blocks which, when rebuilt, achieves the same result - public speaking success. But leave one of the building blocks out and the tower will likely collapse.

Each building block of a speech is important, relying on each other for support, working together to create the perfect result. Taking short cuts or leaving something out may have negative, possibly serious, effects on a speech, which could embarrass the speaker and may tarnish their reputation, or possibly scare them off from ever speaking publicly again. And it is unlikely they will ever be asked to return. What a loss that would be!

Taking care to include all of the building blocks will help to prevent disaster and produce successful results. There are many building blocks required to produce a great result. The main ones we use are: *topic, audience*, the *three Ps*, *rehearsal, visual aids, delivery*, and *feedback* (see Figure 1).

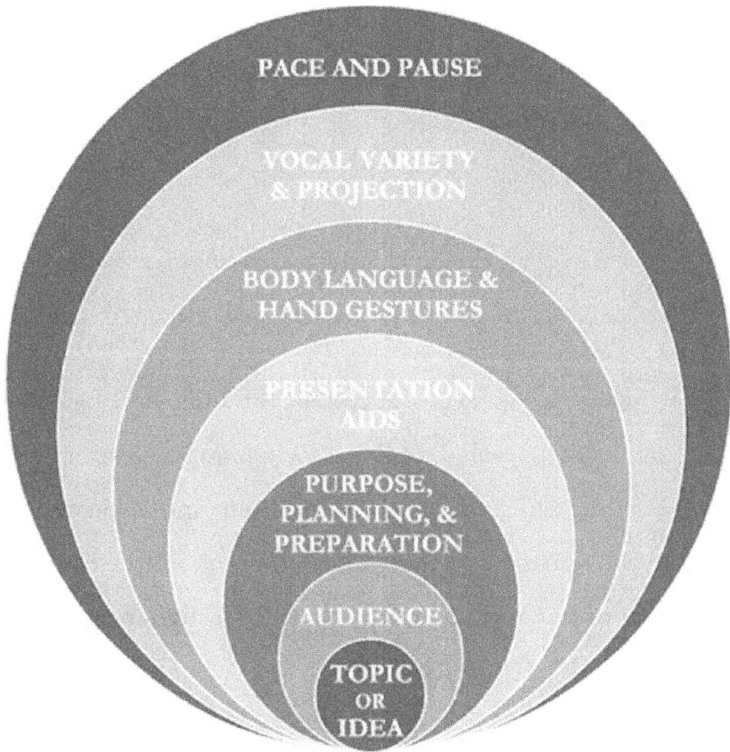

Fig 1: The Building Blocks of an Effective Speech

Public speaking comes in many forms. Perhaps you have been asked to Emcee an event, and have no idea what to do or how to introduce each speaker and guest? As Emcee, you have just become a speaker, yourself! Even as an Emcee, you should deliver a prepared speech, of sorts. Correct planning, preparation, and delivery go into what will become a mini-speech for each speaker or guest you introduce. For more on this subject, refer to Chapter 4.

Effective speakers use verbal and nonverbal communication to convey their message, applying a variety of techniques, such as vocal quality, body language, facial expression, and eye contact, to name a few.

Here we will address the seven critical building blocks you need to consider when creating and delivering an effective speech.

As you read on, you will notice that the building blocks are interconnected – each building block requires reference to other building blocks to determine an outcome or decision – so, always be mindful of this process throughout the planning and execution of every speech, to be an effective speaker.

ONE: Choosing A Topic

"Believe in your ideas and be the best."
Richard Branson

Occasionally, you may be given specific speaking engagements, where the topic is already decided for you and you have a relatively clear idea what your speech will involve. Perfect!

Equally, there will be occasions when you are invited to speak and are required to choose a topic. Speaking about an individual passion, area of expertise, passionate idea or theme, or life experience, may be a no-brainer. Yet, some speakers still struggle or draw a blank when asked to speak about themselves!

Invariably, people suffer with insecurity, often unjustly believing there is nothing in their lives worthy of developing into a speech, especially to a large audience. Unfortunately, that's human nature – self-deprecation, a feeling of incompetence, inadequacy, and low self-esteem – classic signs of diffidence: a lack of confidence. Typically, those thoughts couldn't be further from the truth.

'I can't think of anything to talk about.' 'I've got nothing interesting to say.' 'My life's boring.' 'No one wants to hear what I have to say.' 'I wouldn't know where to start.' These are just a handful of the comments I hear. Each person has a lifetime of experiences, stories, ideas, and thoughts to convey to others, no matter how young or old they are, yet seem to find themselves baffled, even terrified, when choosing something to develop into a speech. Plagued with self-doubt and undervaluing themselves, their stories, ideas, and thoughts would go unheard, if not for the support and encouragement of others. I am constantly delighted and heartened by the genuine surprise my clients experience when delivering their first speech in front of an audience, usually to rousing applause.

The first thing to ask, when choosing a topic, is: who is my audience? This is a strong example of the interconnecting links of the building blocks. Speakers should always be audience-centric, thus when deciding on a topic or idea, will be mindful of their audience throughout the decision-making process.

Choose a topic that interests you and will resonate with the audience. Listeners enjoy hearing about a speaker's interests, life experiences, family life, work life, expertise, ideas, passions, and pursuits and, in turn, it provides a speaker with endless topics and subject matter for speeches. If something is important, i.e., it matters deeply to you, then you should find it easy to talk about. Look at it another way: if you can hold the interest of your audience in general conversation about the topic, you can create and prepare a speech worthy of a larger audience – it just takes more effort. We are all capable of creating a great speech if we are prepared to invest the time and effort.

Still unsure? Consider, for a moment, what you love; what you find yourself talking or thinking about most; what you are passionate about; what idea or suggestion you want to share; what you experienced as a child, an adult, or at work; what challenge you overcame; what inspires you; or anything else that you know inside-out and front to back, that will interest your audience. Therein lies your topic.

Speaking about something you know well, love, or are passionate about and which arouses your deepest convictions, assures it will be easier to plan and deliver your speech and, thereby, instil self-confidence. Your passion will be evident in your delivery, too, which will help to engage, persuade, and motivate your audience. If you're not excited, chances are your audience won't be, either.

However, there may be times when you will be required to deliver a speech on a topic that you know little or nothing about and thus requires research. It is paramount that you avail yourself time to become familiar and comfortable with the topic, before delivering such a speech. Failing to do so, or procrastinating, is likely to convey your lack of knowledge on the topic to your audience which, in turn, may affect your confidence and speech effectiveness. Plan ahead to succeed and avoid embarrassment.

You may be required to pitch a particular product or service, in which case, the topic is already decided for you. There are, of course, ways that you can tweak or adjust your speech to make it more interesting to the audience.

Remember, before finally settling on a topic, you must also consider the second building block: The Audience. Some topics or content may be irrelevant or inappropriate to certain audiences. Once you have established its audience, narrowing down the choice of topic will be much easier to determine.

With a topic decided on, you can develop a *Central Idea*.

Central Idea

What is your central message or idea? What is the point you want to make? This should be a direct, one-sentence statement or declaration that clearly defines your message, not a slogan, phrase, or question.

For example:

☒ Revolutionary, new cleaning product.

☒ Can our revolutionary, new cleaning product help you?

☑ Our revolutionary, new cleaning product cuts cleaning time in half, saves you money, and is environmentally safe.

Now that your central idea is clearly defined, everything else in your speech - the key points (or main ideas) - should support your central idea, i.e., the reasons why your central idea is true.

It is helpful, at this point, to make brief notes on:

- Why you want your audience to hear this message - it is relevant to your audience, it will invoke interest, and listeners will connect with the message.

- How you want your audience to think, feel, or act;

- Which stories, anecdotes, or points to include;

- Develop a 'Call to Action,' if required.

Scope

Having selected the topic and developed the central idea, you may need to narrow its scope; too broad a topic may fail to engage the audience and convey your message. It is crucial to keep within the constraints of your speaking engagement, thereby narrowing your topic to a specific area of importance or interest, though this can sometimes be challenging.

When narrowing your topic, you must consider the purpose of your speech - discussed in detail in sub-chapter Three: The Three Ps.

Here are some examples of the process used to narrow speech topics:

1. **Too broad**: Climate Change

   Less broad: Effects of Climate Change

   Narrowed: Effects of Climate Change on the Arctic

   Best: Global Warming and the Decline of the Polar Ice Cap

The scope of this topic has been narrowed down to a specific issue: how global warming is contributing to the melt of Arctic polar ice caps. Although informative, in this instance, the speaker's purpose is to inspire or persuade the audience to make changes in their everyday lives, to help slow or halt the process of global warming. The speaker would then deliver a conclusion, reinforcing the need for everyone to change their thinking and regular habits, to contribute to saving the ice caps.

2. **Too broad**: Modern Technology

   Less broad: Modern Technology Pitfalls

   Narrowed: How Social Media Can Impact our Lives

   Best: Conquering Cyber Bullying

The scope of this topic has been narrowed down to a specific issue: how to defeat or conquer cyber bullying. In this speech, the speaker's purpose is to create awareness - inform the audience of the issue of cyber bullying and its possible consequences - and offer solutions to the problem. The speaker would then deliver a conclusion, reinforcing the issue and offer or suggest ways to deal with it.

Once you have chosen a topic and narrowed its scope, in keeping with the purpose of your speech, you can move on to the next stage. Remember: be flexible - allow yourself to adapt the speech, if necessary. As your speech develops, you may find yourself drawn toward another angle, leading on a different path and outcome. That's fine, provided you remain within the parameters of the assignment agreed upon, if a specific request has been made.

TWO: Know Your Audience

The average man speaks without thinking;
an intelligent man thinks first.

At every stage of your speech you must be mindful of your audience, i.e., have an audience-centred approach to public speaking. A skilful public speaker invests considerable time researching and planning, to be audience-centric. However, 'Know Your Audience' is an overarching building block, which is constantly being assessed and reassessed, from speech inception, through to conclusion of delivery and applause.

Whilst considering a topic or idea that you want to share with others, ensure it is suitable for your audience. To do this we must first identify our audience. For instance, delivering a speech on 'Achieving Financial Independence for the Over Sixties' would not be particularly relevant to a younger audience; neither would 'Banning Unhealthy Food in Schools' be appropriate delivered to the fast food industry.

How well you and your speech are received by an audience is often determined by the amount of effort you conducted into researching the audience earlier.

It is essential to understand your audience, to enable greater connection and engagement. And, although some may appear similar, no two audiences are identical. Never assume to know an audience without making an effort to find out more about them. Failure to analyse an audience can lead to disaster.

Do some research to find out as much as you can about your audience, including diversity of audience: who they are, how knowledgeable they are, what their expectations are, what they care about, what commonalities you have with them, and what past speakers have spoken about.

Seek as much information as you can to form a background, to assist in planning or adapting your speech to suit your audience. Ask yourself questions, such as:

- Who is my audience?

- What is my audience demographic?

- Is the topic suitable and age-appropriate?

- Is the language or grammar used, suitable?

- Will the topic resonate with my audience?

- Have they heard a similar speech before?

- Do they want to be here – are they friendly or hostile?

- Are they likely to be interactive or reserved?

It is important to research the venue and environment, too, including time of day and audience size. Both speaker and audience can be affected by their surroundings. Often, simple adjustments can be made beforehand to enhance the delivery and reception of a speech.

Simple condition factors can affect both speaker and audience. Am I the first or last speaker of the day? Is the room hot and stuffy? Is the lighting adequate? Are there enough chairs for everyone to be seated? Do I have room to move around and interact with my audience?

Many elements need to be considered. There are far too many to list, but here are some examples:

- How will my audience view me - will I be on stage, out the front of a room, or at a table in a boardroom?

- Is my audience seated or standing?

- Am I expected to be standing or sitting?

- What is the size of the room?

- What is the size of the audience?

- Is there any internal or external noise interference?

- Is a microphone required?

- Are visual aids available, such as a projector & screen?

- Is the room temperature comfortable?

- What time of day will I be speaking?

- Will my audience likely be tired?

- Am I following on from other speakers or events?

Be audience-centric: sensitive to cultural diversity, including ethnicity, religion, age, and gender; conscious of any audience verbal and nonverbal cues to your speech; and make any appropriate adjustments on the fly.

If using a pre-planned speech, be prepared to modify the speech to consider the needs and background of each audience. A great speech for one audience, is not necessarily ideal for another. Simple changes to language or grammar can make a huge difference between an audience's understanding and perception, or complete misunderstanding.

Audience analysis is ongoing - dynamic - so you may need to revise your material as you learn more about them, constantly evolving your speech, as required. You should continue to reassess your audience, whilst moving onto each building block, right up until the conclusion of delivery of your speech.

THREE: The Three Ps

Careful planning, preparation and execution is essential to an effective speech and being a successful public speaker. Each step in the planning and preparation process - determining its purpose, mapping it out, developing the central idea, generating main points, gathering supporting material, choosing a speech style, and organizing the speech - is congruent with its delivery, in order to articulate our message.

As a speaker, your mission is to capture your audience's attention and get them onside - to connect with you or, at the very least, make them mindful of the message, without offending or creating hostility. Therefore, the topic or idea must be made interesting inside the minds of your listeners - the audience - to be effective.

In Chapter 2 we spoke of the three important Ps of a successful *speaker*, *Preparation, Preparation, Preparation.*

Equally, there are Three Ps crucial to every *speech*:

Purpose, Planning, & Preparation

You need to determine the purpose of the speech, then plan and prepare a speech worthy of your audience that reflects their knowledge, interests, and expectations so that your words and actions resonate with them and have the desired effect.

It is important to remember the purpose of your speech throughout the entire planning, preparation, and delivery process, and not lose sight of its objective.

Purpose

The general purpose of a speech is to *inform, persuade, inspire, or entertain* an audience. A speech may, indeed, have elements of more than one purpose, but it's specific, or main, purpose should be clear.

Every successful speech has a specific purpose: to achieve a specific outcome, leaving the audience able to remember, feel, or do what you intended.

Determine the specific purpose of every speech, beginning with the following statement: "At the conclusion of my speech, the audience will be able to ..." The outcome should be observable or measurable: the audience will be able to list, decide, take steps to, ensure, begin, explain, describe, write, order, etc., and limit it to one idea. Multiple ideas lead to confusion and can lack consistency.

The speech should not be centred on you, but be audience-centric. For instance, simply telling the audience about yourself, someone, or something else, might be interesting, but it needs to have specific purpose. Ask yourself, "What do I want the audience to remember, feel, or do?"

If you can't answer that, chances are your audience will have no idea, either. Determining the purpose of your speech early on will clarify your objectives and give you focus, ensuring a more interesting and effective speech.

How do you want your audience to respond?

For example: you are telling your audience about a new, revolutionary cleaning product on the market. Although you are *informing* them of the new product and its benefits, in reality, your purpose is to *persuade* them to purchase the product, once you've concluded your speech. Therefore, you also need to emphasise how the audience will benefit from purchasing and using the product: Statements such as, "It will cut your cleaning time in half, make cleaning easier, cost less, and is environmentally friendly" will have far greater impact and effectiveness than information alone.

Inform: to teach an audience something new, or expand their existing knowledge.

Probably the most common purpose, it is used for a multitude of topics and ideas, such as introducing a new concept, demonstrating a process, reporting project outcomes to management, presenting new objects or products, or teaching new skills.

If care is not taken, a speech to inform can be dull and boring to the listener. Try to keep it light, adding a touch of humour and engaging the audience, where possible.

Persuade: to influence their behaviour or thinking.

Trying to persuade someone to think or act a certain way can be difficult. Audiences are wary, the result of being constantly bombarded with commercials, salespeople, partners, and others, wanting us to follow their way of thinking. Therefore, this type of speech requires careful consideration and planning to win them over, so they like you, respect you, and trust you. They must identify with you in some way, and you must give them a reason why they should listen to, and perhaps act on, what you have to say.

Inspire: to motivate your audience to act on something, or improve themselves, in some way, whether personally, professionally, emotionally, or spiritually.

Again, this type of speech requires careful consideration and planning to win the audience over. The objective is to connect with the listener on an emotional level, challenge and encourage them to do more, and specify the benefits they can expect if they do so. Emotions are contagious, so you need to express emotions well, to 'hook' them.

Entertain: to present a point in a low-key, perhaps humorous way, ensuring the audience has a good time; often used at events, such as weddings, conventions, and seminars, to create an interesting diversion from the formalities and entertain the audience.

Humour can be a powerful way of delivering a message and engaging an audience when it's appropriate. However, humour should always be fun, inoffensive, and non-target-specific, or you risk being perceived as hurtful and unprofessional.

Most humorous speeches do not contain jokes or one-liners. It is the humorous content and the way the narrative is delivered that has your audience relaxed, smiling, and laughing.

Using jokes and one-liners can be hazardous. Unless they are funny and you have a knack for comedic delivery, jokes should be avoided. Otherwise, they can appear over-rehearsed, poorly delivered, and leave the audience cringing. And don't laugh at your own jokes … you may be the only one laughing!

Before embarking on this type of speech, it is essential to identify the audience clearly. For example, if delivering a humorous speech at a function, are they likely to be inebriated? You may need a thick skin!

It is easy to forget or digress from the intended purpose of your speech as it develops, so jot it down and keep it displayed somewhere prominent, as a constant reminder to stay on track.

Planning

Once you have established the purpose, you can begin planning the speech. But remember not to get caught up in the finer details and lose sight of its purpose.

The length of the speech is a key factor to consider here. Whether you have three minutes, seven minutes, or thirty minutes, whatever time is allocated to your speech will determine the amount of narrative and detail you can include.

A short speech may only allow time to focus on the central idea using one example, to achieve the purpose quickly and effectively. A longer speech provides greater opportunity to include more points and expand detail, using examples and anecdotes relating to the central idea.

Mind Mapping

A *mind map* is a very useful tool with multiple applications.

Generally, we tend to take notes or make a list of important things in lineal text – rows and rows of monotonous information that our brain has to decipher. Whereas a mind map more closely resembles how our brain actually functions and is, therefore, very effective.

A mind map is a simple, visual thinking tool that has a natural organizational structure radiating from its centre. It uses lines, words, colours, symbols, and images to organise material and make connections to the main topic.

Mapping out your speech provides assistance with structuring information to better comprehend, analyse, and recall, whilst keeping focus on the central message or idea.

You don't have to be artistic to create a mind map: start in the centre of a blank piece of paper in landscape orientation; write, draw, or paste an image of your central idea; use colour, symbols, drawings, images, varied text, font size, bold, and italics, etc., to connect your main points to your central idea. Repeat the process to connect your sub-points to the main points (see Figure 2 example).

Don't be afraid of ending up with too many main points and sub-points to include in a speech – the mind map will help you to formulate and visualize a plan, as you continue through the development process. This will ensure you only include important and meaningful material, whilst eliminating superfluous guff, to create an appropriate and effective speech for the intended audience. Keep the mind map displayed prominently, so that you can refer to it later.

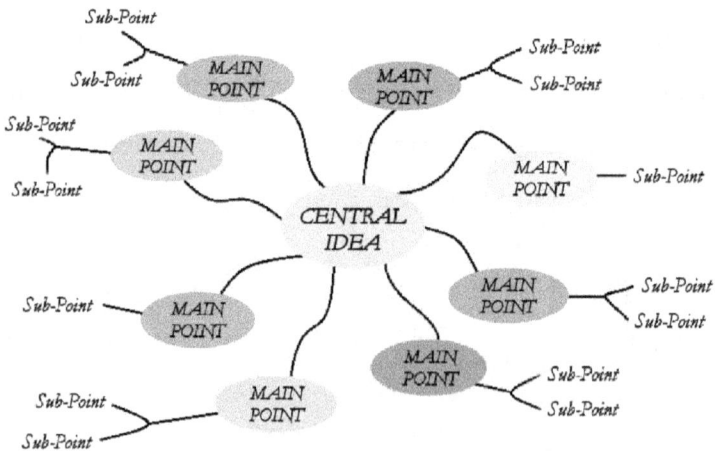

Fig 2: Example of a Mind Map

Think of your speech as a journey: you take your audience along for the ride, guiding them all the way. At this stage, only you know the destination, so it's important to add elements to the journey that relate to it. The journey should be in chronological order, too – it shouldn't jump back and forth – or you risk confusing your audience.

First, establish a *Through-line*.

Through-Line

Noun - a theme or idea that runs from the beginning to the end of a book, film, etc.

Imagine your *Through-Line* as a cord that runs throughout your speech, with each narrative element attached to it, gradually building on your topic or idea.

Your through-line should be at the beginning of your speech and no more than 15 words, telling the audience where you are going. It must contain a strong argument or idea to capture the audience's attention, making them want to hear more. Although not mandatory to mention upfront, like this, it is much easier for your audience to follow you on your journey, if they understand where you are headed.

The through-line should be weaved throughout the speech, to remind the audience of your message, reinforcing the point.

Avoid being predictable, though. Through-lines, such as, 'My life, from rags to riches', 'Take things one day at a time', 'No pain, no gain', and 'A near-death experience made me reassess my life', are banal and tedious. Be different; incorporate unexpectedness; get creative!

Next, plan the *Structure*.

Structure

Verb – arrange in a careful, organized pattern or system; construct according to a plan.

Every successful speech has a clear *Structure*. How you structure your speech determines its effectiveness. A clear, logical structure is helpful to both you and your audience: you remain in control, appearing more confident, and your audience remembers more of what has been said.

As with a comedy act, timing is everything! Where to place specific points, including stories, anecdotes, and examples, is important, so they have the greatest impact on the audience.

Every good story has a beginning, middle, and end, taking its audience or reader on a journey.

The structure of a speech is the same - it consists of three main elements:

Opening, Body, & Conclusion

Opening: captures the audience's attention, offers an overview of what you are going to speak about, and provides a reason why they should listen. Generally, this is something you say, but could be a nonverbal communication to entice the audience and grab its attention.

The opening must be compelling, to hook the audience, making them want to hear more. A lacklustre or boring opening could harm an otherwise incredible speech and, no matter how grand or interesting the body may be, the audience may have already 'switched off'!

In the past, audiences seemed more patient. Speakers were given time to gain a listener's trust, attention, and interest. In the Technological Age, however, audiences can be brutal, allowing speakers only fleeting moments, before tuning out. Numerous studies show that we must now engage an audience in the first few, vital seconds … So, make every second count!

Opening Do's and Don'ts

Firstly, try and refrain from thanking your audience for being there, using openings, such as:

- "Thank you for coming out, tonight, on this cold evening;"

- "What a great audience we have, today;" or

- "It's great to be here."

Not thanking or addressing the audience may sound arrogant, but it is not - they are more interested in hearing your speech, than listening to you thank them. More than likely they have come along willingly and been looking forward to it, anyway. It is also valuable time that is better spent adding to a meaningful speech - the best way to thank your audience.

Secondly, avoid stating how your speech will pan out:

"I'm going to tell you about my experiences with irate customers, and will follow up with techniques you can use when confronted with similar situations."

If you have done your planning and preparation properly, the audience will be able to follow your well-structured speech, without you having to state the obvious at the beginning. Instead, open creatively and powerfully, or with a hook, whilst remembering to incorporate the through-line, to entice the audience to want to hear more.

Finally, revealing your insecurity is counterproductive:

- "You've probably had a long day at work, so it's great to see you could come here, tonight;"

- "I'll endeavour to keep it short;" and

- "I hope you enjoy my speech."

Aargh, stop right there!

You have been asked to speak; you have a right to be there; you know your stuff; people have come along to see and hear you. Stand tall and erect, sense the energy in the room, and feel positively proud.

Again, your planning and preparation will be evident, as you show yourself to be a confident, well-prepared, effective speaker, and they will enjoy your speech. If it is a responsive and good audience, acknowledge this at the end of the speech, simply saying, "Thank you" or "You've been a great audience" - a thoughtful and appreciated gesture.

Body: core of a speech that discusses the main points or ideas and key concepts; provides narratives – anecdotes, examples, facts & figures – of the central topic or idea.

The body usually consists of two or three main narrative points (time permitting) supporting a central theme. Too few points can leave an audience lacking, uncertain, or unconvinced. Equally, too many can leave them feeling overwhelmed, bamboozled, and dazed, and is difficult for them to follow or recall.

Select your main points carefully, choosing those that relate most appropriately with the central theme. Each point should easily and clearly define its relation to the central theme. Your audience should not be left wondering or confused.

Deciding in which order to deliver the main points can be simple to rather complex. Main points:

- May share equal importance and their order of delivery is inconsequential;

- Of an instructional nature generally require a specific order or sequence;

- Based on a sequence of events in time, are usually organised chronologically;

- Ranging from simple to more complex are often delivered in that order, building on the idea or message, aiding an audience's learning - in much the same way we learn at school;

- On a controversial subject, may be received by a hostile audience, in which case leading with the most important point helps to avoid alienating the audience which, in turn, may be more receptive to the rest of the speech. An unfamiliar topic is introduced in the same manner.

Remember, the through-line is the cord to which each of the points are attached, so it is essential they communicate your message effectively.

Conclusion: delivers an important final impression, enabling an audience to hear compressed, or bite-sized, pieces of information regarding the major points and recognise how to apply them to their own experience; verbal or nonverbal cues signify the speech is at an end.

The conclusion must not introduce new information to the audience; it is used to summarise the speech and provide closure; presenting new information defeats this purpose and will confuse listeners.

Avoid using words, such as, "In conclusion, ..." and "In summary, ...". If you plan your conclusion correctly and effectively, your audience will know you have reached the end.

Occasionally, before you arrive at the end of the journey with your audience, it may not always be clear how your speech relates to them, personally. However, a well-planned and executed conclusion makes this clear, finalising the speech to achieve its purpose in a brief, but memorable way. It summarises the main points, referring them back to the central idea; restates the through-line, tying everything together; and leaves the audience onside and able to take the thought-provoking, abstract information provided and apply it to their own lives. In this manner, the audience will remember how your speech affected them, more than its content - a very effective method to use.

The conclusion generally includes an important message, or a 'Call to Action,' motivating listeners to act or respond in some way. When an audience feels personally involved or affected, they are more likely to act or respond to the message. This can be achieved using illustrations, earlier statistics, personal references, quotations, inspirational appeal, and so on.

Q&A: asking questions allow listeners an opportunity to converse with a speaker and clarify any queries they may have.

When planning question time following a speech, it is often good practice to advise the audience early on that questions will be taken at the end of a speech, if time permits. This helps avoid hands being raised during the speech. However, if it happens, control the situation by politely asking the listener to hold their question till the end. Don't forget to return to the person's question, when question time begins.

Once you have delivered your conclusion, and if time allows, reward the audience by offering question time. Avoid questioning the audience: "Are there any questions?" Instead, use well-formulated sentences, such as, "I'd now like to open the floor to any questions." Pause for around 10-15 seconds. In the event of no forthcoming questions from the audience, you could pose a question and answer yourself, to get the ball rolling. Fill the 'silence' void by being prepared: have a brief scenario or question and answer to use, particularly one that refers to the 'Call to Action.'

For example: "You're probably thinking, 'Where do I start?' A good place to begin would be …"

Having finished answering your own question and there are still no audience questions forthcoming, you've clearly done a great job presenting your topic and it is time to wrap up with a brief statement, encapsulating your message: "I'll leave you with this thought ...", thus ending your speech on a strong note.

Research & Intel

Researching and gathering supporting material is essential for most, if not all, speeches. Supporting material provides evidence, such as facts, definitions, statistics, and quotes, which invariably forms the basis of, or offers, examples relevant to the speaker's particular audience.

There is also a multitude of nonverbal, visually stimulating information available to research that will assist you in planning and delivering your speech, such as photographs, video, charts, and graphs. Determine which material is most valuable and use it where suitable to support your message. For example, a lengthy explanation of a point may be required, but could be replaced with a single graphic encapsulating the point, speaking volumes, stirring an audience's emotions.

Think about and plan your speech from your audience's perspective – use descriptions and explanations to help them understand a point, and offer facts or illustrations to raise awareness or evoke emotion - emotions are contagious.

Use content that resonates with your audience – if they can identify with the story or information, they will feel connected and engaged with you on a personal and emotional level. Include vivid descriptions to allow your audience to mentally visualize what you're saying.

Anecdotes or personal experiences are extremely effective at engaging an audience, keeping them interested, and appealing to their emotions. Brief stories or illustrations, which are linked, tend to have more impact than one long story, as they demonstrate a pattern or trend. However, if a longer story is compelling, with a well-developed opening, problem, climax, and resolution, the audience is likely to be engrossed, as they are taken on the journey to learn the outcome.

Hypothetical situations and examples can be used, but never attempt to fool your audience into thinking the event occurred. It is best practice to introduce the hypothetical situation for what it is.

For example:

"Imagine someone ..."
"How would you feel if ...?"

It is not necessary to introduce a story with, "Let's look at this hypothetical situation as an example …" unless it is unclear to the audience that the illustration is a hypothetical one.

Speech intel must be obtained from a credible source – reference books, research papers, newspapers & periodicals, personal experience, internet. Once credibility is established, *always* credit your source:

- ☒ "We cannot solve our problems with the same thinking we used when we created them."

- ☑ "As Albert Einstein once said, *We cannot solve …*.'"

- ☒ "About one trillion single-use plastic bags are used annually around the globe. That's nearly 2 million every minute."

- ☑ "According to the website, earth-policy.org, *'About one trillion …*.'"

As you do your research, take notes and record where information and material were obtained, so you can easily refer back to it, if needed. Anything that has been obtained from another person or place, including such things as quotations, pictures, statistics, publications, and data, whether used in full, in part, or paraphrased, you must *always* quote the source. You will be viewed as knowledgeable and trustworthy for exhibiting such honesty.

It is generally accepted a speaker will, from time to time, offer his opinion on a particular subject or point he is speaking about. However, it is only acceptable when the speaker declares the information is exactly that, their own opinion, not fact, using, "I believe ..." or "I feel ..." and so on. And never attempt to mislead an audience by making something up, unless you have already made it clear to the audience you are using hypothetical examples and situations.

In some speeches, figures and statistics are important elements to include in a speech to emphasise the message, but are often used ineffectively, overwhelming the audience, or getting 'lost in translation'. For example, "More than 3,000 Australians died by suicide in 2017." In this manner, the statistic has little impact on the listener.

However, by relating statistics to something tangible that an audience can visualise, the message becomes more relevant and easier to understand and recall: "According to Life in Mind Australia, over 3000, or the equivalent of more than 52 bus loads of Australians, died by suicide in 2017." For emphasis you might add, "That's equivalent to one bus load of passengers suiciding *every* week!" Even adding, "That's almost 9 people *every* day!" Remember to always quote your source.

Your message adds impact when the words used are visually powerful – tell your audience by painting them a picture. Using the same example in a different scenario: "Australia continually runs a major campaign to reduce the road toll. Imagine if two whole families were being killed on our roads every day. The country would be in uproar. Yet, the equivalent of two whole families are committing suicide every day - we must act now to prevent this from happening!"

Although some material may be interesting and appear to support your central idea, it should be relevant to your specific purpose and audience, otherwise it is superfluous. Be objective: assess the information you gather to support your speech; only use information that is relevant to your purpose *and* that resonates with your specific audience; and remove unnecessary guff. If using a mind map, update it accordingly.

You are now ready to begin crafting your speech.

Preparation

It is often at this point that a speaker feels overwhelmed, gets distracted, or becomes complacent, and finds themselves procrastinating – putting off the inevitable. Then, suddenly realising they're just days, or worse, hours, away from having to deliver their still-unfinished speech, they rush to pull something together, doing themselves and their audience a major injustice!

In reality, it is pointless delivering a speech if the message is lost, poorly explained & delivered, or confuses its listener, failing to be delivered effectively, due to lack of preparation.

The amount of preparation required is dependent on your knowledge of the topic and the time available. You might be lucky enough to be given considerable lead time for preparation, but this is not always the case, so always use time wisely.

Can proper preparation really make that much difference? Absolutely! Preparation will increase your confidence, enhance delivery & audience reception, and help ensure your message is conveyed, thereby improving the effectiveness of the speech.

Inadequate preparation can cause too many problems to list here, but it is safe to say, avoid it at all costs!

Let's now look at the basics of what you must do to prepare your speech, and yourself, for successful delivery.

Writing

With your speech mind map to guide you, allow yourself to be creative, jotting down anything that springs to mind. Don't be concerned about being messy and disorganised at this stage – it's about the thought process, for now, and gathering as much information down on paper to translate into a speech later.

Use the research and intel previously gathered to expand each main point and sub-point of your mind map. Once completed, it should become clear which main and sub-points strongly support the central idea and most effectively convey your message – these are the ones to incorporate into your speech; cull the rest. I know, it's not easy, but it must be done.

Be succinct, omitting unnecessary detail, which can otherwise irritate an audience and may cause your speech to be too long.

We often feel there is so much we want to include and don't want to leave anything out, that we forget what is really important – engaging our audience. But information overload can cause listeners to be bored, confused, overwhelmed, disengaged, or worse, leave!

Include only what is important – that which correlates to the central message or idea and suits the purpose – everything else is unnecessary. It may be difficult to do, but is essential.

If you have additional information, products, services, etc., that you want your audience to be aware of, you can offer these as an adjunct, aside from your speech, and before concluding:

"These revolutionary cleaning products are just three of the many environmentally friendly products we stock. Come and see me during the break and I will be happy to discuss our other products, or feel free to sign up to receive a full product list via email."

However, be careful not to dismiss your central idea by being overly concerned about including 'add-ons' or omitting something. In the example above, your audience may become more focussed on finding out what they haven't heard about, rather than the central idea you were trying to present.

Unless planning a formal speech, such as a ceremonial speech using a manuscript, avoid writing the speech out in full, or you will be tempted to read or memorize it. Write the speech outline, only. Use each outlined point and write a key word or brief phrase to jog your memory of what you will talk about at each stage of your speech. Using notes in this manner allows freedom of creativity and less rigidity, which comes across as stiff.

Present the topic using examples, anecdotes, facts & figures, or stories, which remind the audience of the message and provide opportunities to inject your through-line.

Mark your transition to each main point, from one to the next, using verbal or nonverbal cues, marking them as such in the outlined speech, if necessary. However, numbering each point aloud, sounds juvenile. Moving purposefully on stage, such as stage-left, centre-stage, stage-right, helps an audience identify the nonverbal transition between main points. For more on this, refer to the next sub-chapter – Four: Rehearsal.

Involve the audience, or at least its thinking. Use rhetorical questions to engage. For example, "How would you feel if someone handed you $10k cash? Now amplify that amount 100 times over. You now have $1m in your hands. How would you feel now? What could you do, what *would* you do, with all that money? It's a wonderful thought, isn't it?" … Pause briefly following each question, allowing the audience time to contemplate, but not too long that people call out their responses. Be prepared for the occasional blurted out answer by planning a fitting response.

Consider using words to identify a time, era, place or similar, of each point, which clearly marks the separation and is recognised by the audience. Avoid terms that will disengage an audience, such as, "In conclusion", "Finally", or "Lastly". Audiences tend to 'tune out' hearing this.

Remember: do not try to write your speech out in full and memorise it word-for-word. This can sound over-rehearsed, and if you forget your lines or lose your place, you can come unstuck and your authenticity will likely suffer.

Language

Use appropriate language and grammar for the expected audience. The language and grammar you choose for one audience may not necessarily suit another audience, as discussed earlier. A layperson may find your message confusing if the language is too technical or specialised; conversely, a knowledgeable, technologically-minded audience will cringe if every minute detail is explained.

The use of ***abstract*** or ***concrete*** words will appeal differently to your audience:

- ***Abstract*** or figurative language refers to intangible qualities or ideas, is vague, and can be easily misinterpreted.

- ***Concrete*** language is specific, literal, and tangible and appeals to our five senses – this offers clear communication to an audience.

This example demonstrates evolving from abstract to concrete:

Dog – working dog – sheep dog – Australian Kelpie

Language is complex and speakers must be understood by their audience, or they will not achieve their purpose. Use simple words, which an audience can easily comprehend. Replace long, complex words with shorter, simpler words that have the same meaning and emphasis.

Use every day English language, where possible. It may sound impressive using foreign phrases, such as Joie de vivre, but not everyone knows it means vitality, or enthusiasm for life. And it can make the speaker appear pompous.

Only use words you are familiar with: that you know and use regularly, in correct context, can pronounce correctly, and fully understand their meaning. Using words and phrases incorrectly is exasperating to an audience, as is modern, 'text-speak' to the older generation, who are often oblivious to its meaning, and may cause them to lose interest and 'switch off.'

Use appropriate, unbiased, and inoffensive language; avoid language that may be considered offensive, defamatory, risqué, or derogatory.

When using Metaphors, Similes, Alliteration, Personification, and Short Sentences, understand their meaning, appropriateness, and possible impact on the speech:

- Metaphor - A figure of speech containing an implied comparison, as if one and the same.

  Examples: Life is a rollercoaster.

- Simile - A figure of speech making a comparison between two things, using 'like' or 'as.'

  Example: The night fell, black as despair.

- Alliteration - using the same letter or sound at the beginning of adjacent or closely connected words.

  Example: Little Lucy loves licking lemons.

- Personification – Giving human characteristics to an animal, object, or idea.

  Example: The plants were begging for water.

- Short Sentences - Express significant thoughts: simple words can have as much impact as a longer sentence.

  Example: They came at dawn.

Be creative: show your story, don't tell it. Paint a visual picture with words that demonstrate ideas and thoughts, rather than using declarations. 'Showing' an audience through vivid words, thoughts, actions, senses, and feelings, rather than simple descriptions or statements allows them to experience the story:

Telling: It was freezing outside and the young boy was drenched from the rain.

Showing: The bitter cold nipped at the boy as he stood outside, saturated from the pouring rain.

Editing

Editing is often one of the hardest parts of preparation for a speaker, as they may have devoted a great deal of passion, energy, and time on the speech already and, invariably, believe *everything* is important and needs to be kept. Speakers can be very possessive of their writing and detail, not wanting to relinquish any of it and being impractical or unrealistic about the content. In fact, some feel they have donated their 'life-blood' into their speech!

However, we should always remember:

'At every stage of a speech we must be mindful of our audience.'

Be succinct! Don't wattle, say only what is necessary for the point to be understood and the message conveyed.

Scenario: Imagine yourself a police officer. A man walks into the Police Station immediately following a theft to report the crime. You ask him to explain how the theft occurred. The man then launches into a lengthy spiel about two occasions, years ago, when he'd thwarted a would-be thief, eventually finishing his tale with details of today's theft.

Outcome: Whilst the stories are perhaps interesting and similar, unless the offender was the same person on each occasion, the earlier stories are unrelated and of no real significance to you, as a police officer, reporting on the current crime. As his audience, you were subjected to unnecessary and unrelated information, wasting your valuable time, and you may have completely disengaged from the speaker's message.

Be objective: remove any superfluous sections; tighten and correct grammatical errors; and time the speech to ensure you do not go over time, or too far under, and adjust accordingly.

My golden rule of editing is: only say what needs to be said to convey the message succinctly. In other words, trim or expand where necessary, to communicate an idea effectively. A great speech has a clear and concise opening, body, and conclusion. It is very easy to go off on a tangent, get distracted by a great story, lose your way, or bombard the listener with 'too much information.' It is important to ensure your speech stays true to its intended purpose.

Read & Revise

Hearing your speech can throw a whole new perspective on it – you will likely view it in a different light. Countless speeches have been totally revamped, or even binned, once heard aloud for the first time. Practising or reading aloud provides an opportunity to *hear* what is being said - this auditory recognition affords greater understanding and a sounder perspective of what the audience will likely experience.

Recording and playing back your speech is an even better method to use. If you have a smartphone or laptop/PC camera & microphone, utilise the benefits by recording yourself practising or reading the speech aloud. As you listen to the recording, you may hear particular words, phrases, or clichés you feel should be changed or removed, or perhaps identify sub-points that don't have the desired impact, or are lacking and need enhancement, which might otherwise have been missed when simply practised or read silently to yourself.

Once you have finalised the reading & revision process, move on to rehearsal and use the recording device as an audio/visual tool to help perfect your delivery.

Don't be surprised if, during rehearsal, you make more revisions to the speech – this is common.

FOUR: Rehearsal

*"When we get together and rehearse ... we always talk about
what would make it better, what would mean more,
what would say more. So, we're always improving and growing."*
Alice Cooper

The importance of rehearsing a speech cannot be overstated
but is often overlooked or dismissed entirely by a speaker.

A great speech on paper can still fail, if the speaker neglects to
prepare its delivery, i.e., a disastrous delivery will unlikely save
even the best-written speech! The speaker will lose credibility
and alienate the audience. Equally, an ineffective speech can be
elevated, somewhat, by an effective delivery. Audiences are
inclined to believe what they see more than what is said.

The four basic methods of delivery are:

- Impromptu - off the cuff; this method affords no
  opportunity to rehearse; unless practised in the
  technique of impromptu speaking, such speeches usually
  lack research and organization.

- Manuscript - reading the speech in full; this method is
  generally reserved for ceremonial & other extremely
  formal occasions, statements to the press, or when exact
  wording is essential.

- Memorised - recited verbatim; this method can appear over-rehearsed or stilted; speakers often come unstuck when forgetting their lines. It is best left to thespians.

- Extemporaneous – written or memorised outline, key ideas, and organized structure, often delivered in a conversational style; this method is ideal, as it appears dynamic and natural, rather than artificial and forced.

Practising the content of your speech, the delivery method, and delivery style, and ironing out any problems, is a must for any successful speaker. Imagine attending an unrehearsed play and witnessing the inevitable mistakes, hiccups, or forgotten line; the show would be spoiled, leaving the audience extremely underwhelmed. And very likely, annoyed! No director on earth worth his salt would have actors appear on stage in front of an audience, without having rehearsed multiple times – you should treat delivering a speech with the same respect.

Public Speakers should treat each speech and its audience with respect and afford the same quality of rehearsal.

However, as mentioned in an earlier chapter, do not try to memorise your speech verbatim - unlike a play, in which reciting the script in full is often crucial to the plot or another cast member's cue - as reciting it word-for-word can appear stilted and unnatural, and you may come unstuck or lose your place if you forget a word or line.

You want to appear well planned and confident in your delivery - learning the introduction and conclusion thoroughly will help.

Knowing the intro well gets you off to a great start, assisting in settling any nerves, giving you more confidence, and helps you to remember the gist of your message, leading you into the main points (or body) of your speech.

Knowing the conclusion well enables you to wrap up your speech and remind the audience of the important message and, if applicable, the 'Call to Action.'

It may feel strange at first, delivering to an imaginary audience, but try to push that feeling aside and concentrate; fooling around, or not taking rehearsal seriously, is a waste of valuable time.

Be genuine and rehearse authentically: imagine you have a real audience listening and deliver your speech accordingly!

For example, if you plan delivering the speech:

- Standing - rehearse standing, not sitting;

- In an auditorium – rehearse in a large room or hall, not a small room or office;

- Using a microphone – practise with a microphone; if using a handheld microphone, be conscious of not gesturing with the hand holding the mic, as your voice will trail off;

- Using visual aids – practise using them; determine where materials will be placed before and after use. If using technology, such as slides on a PowerPoint show, have a backup plan, should the technology fail … it just might!

Rehearsing your speech is vital in order to recognise important factors, such as timing, as well as verbal and nonverbal communication, including pace, pause, emphasis, tonality, projection, body language & gesturing, stage presence, use & effect of visual aids, and more.

Many other factors contribute to a great delivery, including facial expressions, eye contact, vocal variety – the power of voice - an audience-centric approach, and, of course, being yourself! These factors are separated into two categories: *nonverbal communication* and *verbal communication*.

Let's take a look at each category.

Nonverbal communication

Listeners believe more of what they see than what they hear. Therefore, whilst the message is important, a speaker cannot rely on verbal communication alone to deliver an effective speech.

There are nonverbal tools you can use to enhance your speech, which will attract your audience's interest and attention in a positive way. Nonverbal communication is very important, too, and should be used to complement verbal communication. But they must never contradict each other.

Essentially, both nonverbal and verbal communication contribute to speech and speaker effectiveness, therefore, they deserve equal effort.

Nonverbal messages should appear natural, effortless, inoffensive, and varied, and coincide with the chosen method and style of delivery. This takes practice to perfect.

Be authentic! Do not try to trick an audience by masking or faking how you feel, as it has a habit of presenting itself in a variety of ways, from a change in vocal pitch to blushing to excessive sweating, and an audience *will* notice!

Clothing

Dress for the occasion. It may seem insignificant compared to the content and delivery of your speech, but what you wear can have a profound effect on how you are perceived.

First impressions count! Your audience is likely to give you kudos for making an effort and you will be held in higher regard, more so than someone who arrives inappropriately dressed – their attention may be drawn to the unsuitable apparel, rather than the speech. – creating a negative response before you've even begun to speak!

It doesn't mean you need to wear a suit, corporate attire, or glitzy dress each time. For instance, a formal speech delivered in a corporate setting would normally demand formal attire, whereas casual or relaxed clothing would be suitable for an informal speech delivered to students.

Dress appropriately, befitting the audience and occasion. If unsure, ask the organiser.

Stage Presence

Noun: the ability to command the attention of an audience by the impressiveness of one's manner or appearance.

How you present on stage matters – it plays a vital role in speech delivery. After all, why would an audience want to listen to you – what makes you worth listening to? Making a good impression immediately you enter the stage will likely make an audience sit up and want to hear what you have to say.

Stage presence equals the sum total of all the qualities a speaker displays, drawing an audience in, commanding its full attention; an audience will remain fully engaged throughout and is inclined to remember the speech and speaker well, thus contributing to a highly effective speech.

Such qualities include:

- charisma, charm, and confidence, including appearance, comfort, attitude, and posture; body language; hand gestures; facial expressions; eye contact; and choreography & use of stage;

- tone of speech – vocal variety, pace & pause, and humour.

Again, first impressions count. These first impressions can strongly influence ongoing judgements about a speaker.

Your appearance, then, matters. A seemingly arrogant, uncertain, apologetic, or negative attitude; stooped shoulders or hanging head; late, flustered, sweaty, or dishevelled appearance; or inappropriate dress; these and more will influence how you are received.

Make the experience a positive one, beginning with yourself. Walk on stage with confidence, even if you're trembling inside. But don't swagger - you want the audience to sense confidence, not arrogance. Your posture should be erect and facial expression befitting the speech to come. Use common sense. For example, if your speech is a sombre one, avoid a broad smile or cheesy grin.

Be comfortable on stage and show it. The audience will warm to you and want to listen. When a speaker walks on stage exuding confidence, an audience is likely to view his comments more favourably than an insecure speaker's. Remember: they have come to see you and want you to succeed.

Occasionally, you may be asked to deliver a speech whilst seated, perhaps at the front of the room, or on stage, or even around a boardroom table, in which case, it is imperative you rehearse in a seated position, so that you are aware of how a seated delivery style affects your speech and are able to make any necessary adjustments.

Depending on the circumstances and environmental factors, you may even choose a seated delivery, particularly in informal arrangements, casual presentations or events, extended presentations, and long Q&A sessions. There are a few things to consider:

- Is the setting casual enough for this style of delivery?

- Is the topic suitable for a more relaxed delivery?

If so:

- Ensure a seated arrangement is approved by organisers;

- Decide whether a stool or chair is appropriate; and

- Discuss with the Emcee when and where you want the stool or chair positioned.

You may also be considering only bringing a chair or stool on stage at the end of the speech, just before commencing a Q&A session. The action of seating yourself prior to a Q&A session relaxes an audience - it senses a change to a more comfortable, conversational setting with you - making listeners more inclined to freely ask questions.

Stage Movement & Transitioning

Where you position yourself on the stage, whether you are stationary or moving around, and how you can use the stage to your advantage, is important to practise during rehearsal. It will soon become clear what works best and what to avoid.

Positioning yourself at various points on the stage to address the audience, particularly if large, keeps listeners attentive, connected, and engaged, and their focus remains on you. However, always move with purpose: avoid walking aimlessly up and down the stage. Altering stage position to represent a transition between main points is a clear indicator to an audience that the speaker is moving on to the next phase of the speech.

Body Language and Hand Gestures

Body language and hand gestures can often make or break a speech - the unspoken word is as effective as the spoken word - so it is crucial to understand when and where to use them in your speech to optimise their effectiveness.

When rehearsing your speech, consider the content and perhaps replacing some words or dialogue using body language or hand gestures, where appropriate, i.e., moments in a speech where words are best left unsaid. A body movement or hand gesture (action) speaks volumes and words are not necessary, especially when combined with an appropriate facial expression, as discussed shortly.

Only use body language and hand gestures where necessary - when it will enhance the speech. Body language and hand gestures should be used to augment the speech, or where words are less likely to express the true meaning of what is being said.

However, it is crucial that it appears natural - don't force it - if it looks and feels right, do it; if it looks or feels odd, uncomfortable, or staged, don't. Overdone or over-acted movements and actions appear false to both the audience and speaker and will likely distance the listener, causing them to be disengaged and aloof.

Be conscious of movements - repeated one-handed, or double-handed, shaking motions; hand-clasping; hands joined at the fingertips; hands together, as if in prayer; finger-pointing; hands-on-hips or in pockets; thigh-slapping; resting one foot on heel, toe pointing forward; walking aimlessly around, or glued to one position on stage, etc. - which can irritate an audience and/or reflect a speaker's lack of confidence and preparation.

Facial Expression and Eye Contact

It is said, 'a picture paints a thousand words,' and so, too, do our faces: just a single expression - a smile, frown, smirk, raised eyebrow, squint, screwed-up nose, poking tongue, pursed lips, wide eyes, wink, and such - tells the audience so much, without a word being spoken.

The benefit of delivering a speech in person to a viewing audience, as opposed to a listening audience, such as over the radio, audio blogs & podcasts, is we can *see* the speaker's face.

Every expression, no matter how small, is discernible to an audience, so make it count! But *always* be natural.

Facial expressions *must* correlate to the words uttered. For example, a sad expression, when relating a solemn event; a smile when telling a happy tale, and so forth. Sometimes, words are superfluous - a facial expression alone is 'enough said.'

The expressions you use to relate your story help an audience to appreciate the message and identify with you.

The same applies when delivering a speech without a visible audience, such as over radio, audio blogs & podcasts: as the muscles in your face produce a smile, sad expression, shock, etc., to complement the story, the emotion is more easily detected by the listener.

Maintaining eye contact with the audience throughout the speech is important, too. Have you ever had a conversation with someone unable to look at you, or meet you eye-to-eye, while they speak? It can be quite disconcerting and, at times, unnerving or even irritating. An audience will also feel this way. People like to feel as if you're speaking to them, and them alone, and making eye contact helps achieve this.

Constantly glancing up at the ceiling or down at the floor gives the impression the speaker is unprepared, seeking answers, or trying to pluck lines of their speech from the ceiling or floor. An audience may sense the speaker's nervousness and lose interest or faith in what they have to say.

Avoid 'hosing' your audience - constantly looking from one side to the other - glancing left to right to left, continually, much like using a fireman's hose.

'Segmenting' the audience is a rather effective technique often used by speakers: directing your attention toward one area of the audience for perhaps 5-10 seconds, before moving your attention to another area. Don't be a slave to rules, though –

just because 5-10 seconds is up, don't feel you *have* to move on — when it feels right, *then* move on.

Try occasionally holding one person's gaze momentarily, to engage them, individually, before moving your gaze to another person or area of the audience; focussing on one audience member at a particularly poignant or powerful moment of the speech is incredibly empowering and the audience loves it!

Each of these actions help to connect and engage an audience, instilling a sense of exclusivity – audience members feel as if you were speaking to them alone!

Verbal communication

Listeners want to *hear* the message delivered effectively, too. A great speech delivered in a droning voice is painful to listen to - an audience will be desperate for it to finish, or perhaps leave!

There are verbal communication tools you can use to enhance your speech, which will attract your audience's interest and attention in a positive way.

Don't try to fake it. Again, be authentic! Verbal communication should appear natural, effortless, inoffensive, and varied, and relate to the speech, which takes practice to perfect.

Vocal Variety & Projection

The Power of Voice – your channelling medium - gives your speech the avenue with which to impart itself upon the listener, enabling the message to be well-received and retained.

Vocal Variety

Noun - a term used to describe variations in the sounds created by speaking, to convey its meaning or intent.

When we communicate with each other, our voices are generally animated, incorporating volume, pitch, light & shade, timbre, cadence, quality, inflection, emphasis, and modulation. Often, and perhaps unconsciously, we simply change the tone and add inflection or emphasis at certain points for dramatic effect. Delivering a speech is no different. You want to keep your audience interested and enthralled - adding these qualities to your delivery helps to achieve this result. We have an amazing arsenal of natural tools at hand, so why not use them?

Imagine talking on the phone to family or friends: picture how animated your voice becomes to interpret specific emotions.

Now envisage how dreary delivering a speech in monotone would be with no change in intonation, inflection, or cadence; great, if your audience is trying to catch some shuteye!

Humans are capable of using an incredible vocal range to reflect feelings, mood, and expressions. Listening to a person speak, we have certain expectations, too: if the story is a happy one, the voice is usually in a mid to high tone or pitch; an exciting story uses a much higher tone; conversely, a solemn story is associated with a much lower, or sombre, tone.

Our voice should reflect the content of the speech: think about what you're trying to convey with words and use the appropriate pitch, emphasis, tonality, and projection.

The following example, using the statement, "The teacher yelled at me," demonstrates how simple variances on where the emphasis is placed in each statement can reflect a change of message or subject:

1. "The *teacher* yelled at me" – in this case, the teacher is clearly the subject of controversy (perhaps due to shock or criticism).

2. "The teacher *yelled* at me" – here, the fact that the teacher yelled is the subject of discussion.

3. "The teacher yelled at *me*" – finally, it is clear the subject lies around the audacity that I (me) was yelled at by the teacher!

In each instance, the emphasised word would be delivered in a higher pitch or tonality; voice projection may also be stronger, to nail home the point.

Projection

Noun - the ability to make a sound heard at a distance.

Vocal projection is important to every speaker: without it, their message may go unheard, captured only by those within close proximity. For the rest, it might as well fall on deaf ears!

Vocal projection is an art in itself: the ability to speak loud enough for the voice to be heard in every part of the room so that each listener can hear you.

It does not mean yelling or shouting!

Some speakers struggle with vocal projection, especially speakers with naturally quiet voices. Though, with practice, they are frequently amazed at the possibilities and eventual outcome.

People generally tend to speak from their chest, utilising only the upper part of their body and lungs to propel their voice forward to the listener. However, speaking from the diaphragm aids vocal projection, allowing the voice to carry further, penetrating larger, deeper regions, thereby reaching more listeners.

Each venue where you will be presenting your speech can have a profound effect upon your delivery. It is rare to be presented with perfect conditions. Some venues pose challenges: rooms that are large & expansive, narrow & deep, small & cramped, or high-ceilinged; halls or auditoriums; areas peppered with background noise or interference; outside in the open-air. Each present their own difficulties, so a speaker should be prepared to make suitable adjustments.

Whenever possible, visit and familiarise yourself with the venue prior to your presentation. If this is impractical, ask questions of the organiser – they will expect this, so don't feel awkward about doing so.

Determine the dimensions and acoustics of the room or auditorium in which you'll be delivering your speech and practise delivering to all areas, without shouting to be heard. If practicable, during rehearsal have someone move around in various positions throughout the audience seating arrangement to ensure your voice is clear and audible to all areas.

If you are planning to use a microphone, rehearse with one. The quality of the microphone and how you hold it will dictate its effectiveness. The technical capabilities of audio enhancing equipment ensures an audience is able to hear, often compensating for a speaker's inability to project. But things can go wrong; technology can fail.

Always plan, prepare, and be able to project to an audience, particularly given the unfortunate unreliability of technology. Just ask any professional speaker, presenter, facilitator, or actor, how often technology has failed them, despite rigorously pre-testing equipment, and they have had to abandon the microphone.

As they say in Scouts, "Be Prepared."

Pace & Pause

"The right word may be effective, but no word was
ever as effective as a rightly timed pause."
Mark Twain

The pace at which we deliver a speech, and pauses used during the speech, are crucial to effective delivery. Put simply it is about working out the right tempo for speaking and, once spoken, adding a suitable length pause.

The tempo, or rate, at which we speak can influence the level of impact our speech has on an audience. Finding the correct pace is critical to keeping an audience's attention and delivering an effective speech:

- Too fast - all the sentences appear to roll into one, or the message becomes garbled, leaving the audience feeling breathless and overwhelmed; the audience cannot hope to absorb all the content sufficiently or effectively - often referred to as 'information overload';

- Too slow - each sentence feels as if it's being physically dragged from the speaker, an exhausting process for the audience; it will likely bore or disconnect the listener, who will 'switch off' their attention, fall asleep, or leave!

There may be times when an individual sentence requires faster or slower delivery, to reflect its meaning and have more impact; equally, a change of pace of a particularly poignant, funny, or remarkable statement, sentence, or quote, might be just what the audience needed to regain focus.

Momentary pausing between sentences is important for speakers to gain composure, catch their breath, and prepare themselves for the next part of the speech; it allows an audience a brief moment to interpret what's been said and store it in memory.

Filler and linking words, such as *ah, um, er, and, so, like,* and *you know,* are the curse of many speakers & presenters, but can easily be prevented or eliminated with a momentary pause.

Try this challenge: watch news reporters, presenters, and interviewees on television - you will be astonished at the overuse of filler and linking words used by these professionals, where a simple pause would have sufficed. Beware – once you hear it, you can't un-hear it … sorry! In fact, you'll probably never again be able to watch or listen to a news report without noticing!

The effect of pausing is particularly helpful to achieve dramatic effect, too. Lengthier, or strategic, pauses at specific moments in a speech are used to enhance excitement or emphasise tragedy. The silence helps to punctuate what was said, create impact, and gives an audience time to consider an important point.

Try videoing or recording your speech, then watch or listen to it back, putting yourself in the audience's position, as though hearing the speech for the first time.

Ask yourself:

1. Are you hearing important and related information?

2. Is the speaker breathless, or the information rushed?

3. Are you given enough time to process the information?

4. Are you likely to feel confused or overwhelmed, at the end?

5. Is the delivery appropriately paced for greatest impact?

6. Is the information powerful and relevant to you?

Make any appropriate notations on your outlined speech where adjustments need to be made and practise until it feels and sounds right.

You have now prepared and rehearsed your speech thoroughly and made any last-minute changes necessary. So, let's go out there and deliver it, eh? No! There is still more to consider and incorporate in your delivery.

Timing

In most instances, you will have been assigned a specific length of time to deliver your speech. If you haven't already done so, it is pertinent that you time your delivery during rehearsal so that you can shorten or extend your speech accordingly, to fit within the time allocated.

Keep your speech as close to the allocated time as possible, whilst still allowing yourself some leeway. For example, if allocated a 15-minute timeslot, your speech should be approximately 12-15 minutes long. If your speech lasts just 8 or 10 minutes, the audience and event organiser may feel cheated; a 20-minute speech may tend to drag, whilst annoying the organisers, who are keen to keep the event running on time.

A speaker who revels in the stage time, abusing the privilege by staying too long or, conversely, can't wait to get off stage and under-delivers, will unlikely be asked back!

Using Notes

It is never ideal to use notes - they can hinder a speaker, as well as give an impression of a lack of knowledge or preparedness and, perhaps, insecurity.

However, if giving a formal speech, where exact wording is vital, you may be required to use notes or, perhaps, the entire manuscript, and your audience will often expect this.

Occasionally, it may also be necessary to use notes with a less formal, or informal, speech, particularly if you are struggling to recall important details of the speech. In such cases, the use of brief notes or bullet points of pertinent statistics or facts will help to remind yourself; in turn, this will help calm nerves, enabling your delivery to be more relaxed and informal.

Aside from formal speeches, as previously mentioned, which may require a speech to be written in full, never use an entire speech as notes – if you lose your way during a speech and need to refer to the notes, finding the spot you are up to can take considerable time, which can be embarrassing.

Short, concise notes or prompts to jog your memory are ideal. Standard paper tends to rustle and bend easily and can seriously irritate or annoy an audience. Firm card, or index cards, are suitable alternatives.

Nevertheless, avoid using notes as a crutch – if you know the topic and have rehearsed the speech effectively and sufficiently, you should not need them. Using notes as an alternative to proper preparation is poor justification and your audience deserves better. Remember, preparation is vital!

Be mindful that using notes can also limit your presentation style and stage movement:

- **holding notes** – restricts hand-gestures & body language, without wanting to appear to 'shake' or rustle papers whilst you speak; gives the appearance the speaker is unprepared, lacking in knowledge, or insecure; and can be extremely irritating to an audience.

- **notes on a lectern** - limits stage movement; may cause the speaker to be 'chained' to the lectern, unable to wander too far away, or constantly returning to the lectern to refer to the notes; may result in a speaker unconsciously reading the speech, presenting a stilted delivery; and the lectern may become a speaker's 'security blanket,' or a physical barrier, disconnecting the audience from the speaker.

- **notes on a teleprompter** - may result in the speaker unconsciously reading the speech, presenting a stilted delivery; the speaker may become reliant on the teleprompter, unable to look away for fear of losing their spot; and may disengage the audience, as the speaker's attention is drawn to the teleprompter.

When notes are essential to your speech, there are methods you can employ to minimise the impact they have on delivery. These will be discussed further in sub-chapter Six: Delivery.

Be Yourself

When rehearsing, practise delivering your speech as you intend to deliver it to an audience: standing or sitting; formal or informal; conversational or instructional. Practise with an imaginary audience to connect easily and engagingly, maintaining eye contact throughout.

Experiment delivering your speech in different ways to find the most suited to you and that which you feel gets your message across to the audience. But be authentic! Authenticity earns an audience's trust - the speaker will be better-received.

Relax. Be natural. Be yourself!

Avoid copying others. No matter how impressed you are with another speaker, you should never try to be them or imitate what they do. It will look false and contrived ... you may be perceived as dishonest and untrustworthy!

However, there may be a particular strategy or element of other speakers and presenters that you admire and wish to incorporate in your delivery. That's okay - try it out during rehearsal to see how it appears. If it looks and feels natural, use it; if not, don't!

Videoing & Recording

Each time you practise or rehearse, try filming yourself.

"Ugh, I can't stand my voice or watching myself on video!"

That's normal, few of us like to watch ourselves, so we know it's not an easy thing to do. But it's a surprisingly effective and useful tool to help polish your speech ready for delivery. And you don't need state-of-the-art equipment to achieve this, either!

For this purpose, a smartphone will do the trick.

Videoing yourself during each rehearsal will enable you to assess your delivery and help pinpoint errors, inconsistencies, or duplications of content, which can be worked on or changed. You will also identify any nervous tics or irritations you may be unaware of, and work on eliminating them entirely.

Watch each video carefully:

- Are your body language & hand gestures congruent with your spoken words, or are they unconnected, repetitive, or irritating?

- Do they enhance, or spoil, the speech?

- Do they look smooth & natural, or overacted & false?

- Do you appear relaxed, knowledgeable, and confident, or nervous, uncomfortable, and apprehensive?

- Is there sufficient vocal variety, such as cadence, inflection, and tonality, or is your voice monotone, high pitched, sing-song, or rushed?

- Is your stage presence charismatic, and movement on stage purposeful, or are you nervous, endlessly pacing, walking around aimlessly, or appear glued to one spot?

- Are any visual aids clear, effective, and appropriate, or boring, too wordy, repetitive, or offensive?

- Is the speech interesting, clear, and consistent with its message, or does the message get lost in tedious or excessive detail?

It is a good idea to compare video with audio, to see how well your message is 'heard,' as opposed to 'seen & heard.' To do this, play the video again with your eyes closed. Listening carefully, does the vocal variety, projection, pace, pause, inflection, emphasis, etc., tell the same story?

If you do not have access to video, at least record your rehearsals in audio. Whilst not ideal, audio recordings will at least enable you to listen to your speech and make an appropriate assessment.

FIVE: Aids & Props

Visual aids and props can add value to a speech, where words are insufficient or require supplementing with images or items for the audience to see, touch, or feel. Visual aids can be:

- Two-dimensional – photographs, slideshows, graphs, videos, whiteboard, flipchart, projector, etc.; or

- Three-dimensional – objects or models, people, animals, etc.

They can be used to provide a timeline or sequence of events, add variety and, at times, entertainment, and help to hold the audience's attention.

Visual aids should be simple, uncluttered, appropriate, and easily seen from any position in the audience.

An image or physical prop can 'say' quickly what would otherwise take a long time to describe. Imagine trying to describe the intricacies of circuitry on a computer motherboard. Instead, display a motherboard photograph, or a real motherboard, to the audience, and they can instantly see what you are trying to convey. Using an image or prop in this way will avoid lengthy descriptions or explanations, saving time, that can be used more effectively, elsewhere.

Avoid using aids or props that distract your audience. Showing an object is a good idea; passing the object around the audience could distract them from listening to what you're saying, especially if they're waiting anxiously for it to be passed to them.

Be mindful of the value of your aids and props: only pass something around the audience if it is absolutely crucial to enhancing their understanding or acceptance of it. Instead, consider inviting them to come and see the item once the speech is over, if they wish to view it more closely.

Most slide shows and PowerPoint presentations are considered dull and boring to an audience - the phrase, 'Death by PowerPoint' was understandably coined - and should be avoided, wherever possible. A few specific slides to reinforce key ideas or points can be useful in a speech, to help the audience retain essential information. But a seemingly endless supply of slides with extensive graphics or text is mind-numbing. Even worse, is when a presenter 'reads' the text on each slide, almost verbatim!

Show & Tell: when showing an image, tell the related portion of the story or information at the same time, then blank the screen when it's time to move on. Leaving an image on the screen once you have moved on to something else, will appear disjointed and the audience's attention will remain on the image, rather than on you.

Whatever visual aid you use, maintain eye contact with your audience, *look* and *talk* to *them*, not the aid. Presenters are frequently temped to turn their heads away from an audience to look at the projector screen or television, as they cycle through their displays. Their voices trail off to the area behind the stage and, without a microphone, are difficult to hear. Similarly, a speaker looking directly at the object held in their hands, whilst continuing to talk, will likely lose proper projection of their voice.

Trust your aid! If you absolutely *must* check it, stop talking first, look back quickly to reassure yourself, then turn to face the audience again and recommence talking. Do not talk whilst your head is turned away from the audience.

Visual supporting material does not have to be complex —the simplest ones are often the best, e.g., an image, object, model, chart, or graph. Not only are audiences inclined to believe what they see more than what is said, they are more likely to remember it, too.

For example, a speech delivered in 2001 on the alarming rate of suicides may have included the following:

"Suicide is among the three leading causes of death among those aged 15-44 years in some countries, and the second leading cause of death in the 10-24 years age group. These figures do not include suicide *attempts*, which are up to 20 times more frequent than *completed* suicide. Although women are more likely than men to attempt suicide, men are much more likely to succeed."[2]

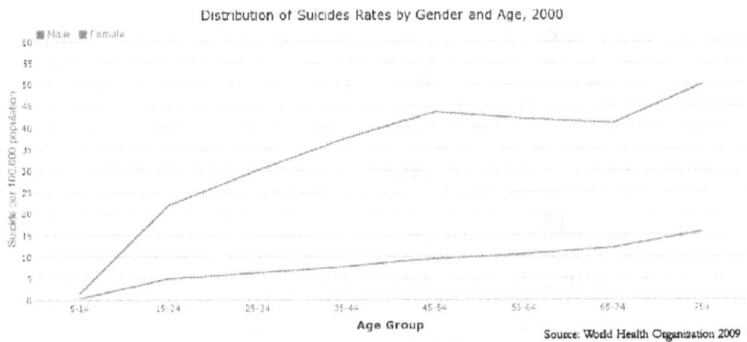

Fig 3: Example of supporting visual material

The chart in Figure 3 shows a drastic contrast in male and female suicide statistics in 2000, worldwide. This brief explanation, accompanied by displaying of the image at the appropriate instant and allowing a moment for the audience to contemplate and absorb its meaning, is far more powerful and impactful than words.

So, too, taking the example given in the sub-section 'Research & Intel' in Chapter 3. In that instance, showing an image of 52 bus loads of people, would be extremely impactful, driving home the message clearly and dramatically.

There may be occasions when a video is useful to enhance a speech or make a point, therefore audio is needed, too. Ensure adequate speakers are positioned appropriately, to guarantee the entire audience can hear what is played. You may also consider using audio alone, to play significant recordings that express a point or convey your message, where visuals are otherwise unnecessary. For example, an inspirational speech may include a portion of John F. Kennedy's speech containing the famous line, "… Ask not what your country can do for you - ask what you can do for your country." Again, make sure everyone in the audience hears it.

Distributing handouts before or during a presentation should be avoided unless it is vital the audience refers to them during the speech, as they create distraction. When reaching the applicable section of your speech, mention the handouts, telling the audience they will be distributed at the conclusion. The audience will look forward to receiving them.

Just as you did when preparing the content of your speech, be mindful of including visual aids, and props, that may distress, offend, or create hostility. For example, some images, videos, or objects, such as graphic images of injured persons or animals, may upset members of an audience, so use them cautiously. If these specific aids or props are essential it is wise to issue a warning before showing them - a tactic often used in the media - providing an opportunity for sensitive or squeamish people to momentarily look away.

Never use threatening or illegal props, e.g., guns, drugs, etc.

SIX: Delivery

By now, you will have gone to a lot of trouble to produce a respectable and purposeful speech. Now it is crunch time!

You are probably feeling nervous, perhaps worrying about many things: what if I get out there and can't speak; what if I can't remember what to say; what if the audience hates me; what if ... what if ... what if? Use this negative energy you're feeling and refocus it – on your message. An audience naturally expects to see a good speech delivered effectively. But they don't expect you to be perfect!

Dispel the fear and embrace the limelight ... this is your moment! Be comfortable in your surroundings. You deserve to be there. You have prepared for this moment, so try to enjoy it as much as possible.

Apply techniques learned in Chapter 2 to manage your fear, e.g., breathing, meditation, etc. Having regularly practised the techniques that are most effective for you, now is the time to apply them.

Tell yourself, "I can do this; I deserve to be here; I know my stuff; I will succeed."

If you are to be formally introduced - by an Emcee, organiser, or such – make sure you have provided them with a brief (15-30 seconds) biography of yourself and the speech, without giving away too much. See Chapter 4 for further details.

Once you have been formally introduced, walk on stage in a calm, confident, and composed manner; look for a smile or a friendly face in the audience, to reassure yourself.

The audience is intelligent. It will sense your comfort and relax itself, ready to listen to your every word. Remember: the audience has invested in you; they have come to see you and want you to succeed!

Prepare yourself and get settled before commencing the speech, i.e., ensuring everything is done before you begin speaking. For instance, if using a manuscript, place it on the lectern; arrange any props on the table, or wherever you have organized; check and adjust the height of the microphone, and make sure it's switched on. Only once everything is ready, should you begin.

Audience-Centric

As an effective speaker, it's not just about being audience-centric when preparing a speech, it's about being audience-centric when during the delivery, too. Don't only focus on the message you're conveying, be receptive to how your audience is responding to the message.

Public speaking is interactive: an audience will listen and provide necessary feedback for the speaker to communicate the message effectively. Being mindful of the audience's response - focussing on reading listeners' receptiveness and attentiveness, such as murmurs, yawns, facial expressions, and nods - is essential to a successful speech. With proper planning and preparation, a speaker is able to identify and remain adaptable to such responses and dynamically alter their speech.

Understanding and recognising changes in mood, reception, etc., enables greater connection and engagement. If audience members appear disinterested, yawn, check their watches, or worse, leave, this reflects adversely on the speaker and signals a need for change. This may mean adjusting any number of variables, such as tempo or rate of delivery, volume, language, use of visual aids, audience participation, and so on. Such awareness and adaptability to make on-the-fly adjustments as necessary, will ensure a well-received delivery and is critical to success.

Remember: avoid rigidity – be flexible. You should constantly evolve the speech, as required. Failing to be flexible and staying on script ensures disaster: you've gone to immense trouble preparing an audience-centric speech; now it's time to deliver it effectively!

Using Notes

On rare occasions, the use of notes will be unavoidable: the formality or complexity of a speech requires the use of a manuscript, or lengthy quotes, comprehensive statistics, or precise details, which require perfect accuracy. In such cases, there are three main methods of using notes, which should be used as inconspicuously as possible:

- **cue cards** – the preferred and least conspicuous method. Use two or three cards, in numerical order, for brief notes or the speech outline, depending on the length of the speech. Cards should be small (fit into the palm of your hand) and unobtrusive; they should be kept in one hand, down by your side, and only referred to when required. This allows stage movement and body language to be unimpeded and your hands able to gesticulate, to enhance your speech.

- **notes on a lectern or teleprompter** – this is the obvious and preferred method when reading from a *manuscript*, freeing up the speaker's hands and body;

although unable to move away from the lectern, if a speaker has practised delivery well, he is able to maintain eye contact with his audience, keeping them engaged and connected to the message. A *teleprompter* has a similar effect, but allows more freedom of movement and, if a lectern is not used, removes the physical barrier between speaker and audience. *Brief notes* - bullet points or cues, such as single words and short phrases - written or printed in a large font and placed on a lectern, can be viewed quickly and from a distance, allowing for freer hand, body, and stage movement.

- **holding notes** – Use small sheets of thin card, size A5 or smaller. Avoid pieces of paper, which tend to rustle. Keep the cards in one hand, allowing freedom of movement of the other hand. If using multiple cards or pages, it is advisable to bind them together, to allow easy page turning and prevent mix-ups & loss of place; *always* number each page; take extreme care not to fiddle or gesticulate with the notes whilst speaking. Use only brief cues, statistics, and such.

SEVEN: Feedback & Review

"It takes humility to seek feedback. It takes wisdom to understand it, analyze it, and appropriately act on it."
Stephen Covey

If you have come this far, you should have already prepared, rehearsed, and delivered your speech. It may have been a wonderful experience, or it may well be something you'd rather forget; either way, you got through it and came out alive. Well done! It's an amazing accomplishment.

First of all, realise what you've achieved and congratulate yourself. Say out loud how amazing and proud you are of yourself – let yourself hear it. You have come a long way. Don't focus on how nervous you were – your confidence will improve with practice.

Now it's time to reflect on what went well, and what can be improved. Was the speech a success - did you get the message across; did the speech achieve its purpose; what worked and what didn't; and how did you feel afterwards: ecstatic, relieved, horrified, or somewhere in-between?

Feedback from the audience is an invaluable tool, and we discuss it in details, shortly. Self-assessment or self-feedback is helpful, too. Reviewing ourselves and the speech can be difficult, but it must be done honestly and effectively, without being overly critical. Don't expect everything to be perfect, especially if this is the first time you've publicly delivered a speech. The idea is to gain as much experience as possible, learn from every experience, and improve each time, until you become a great speaker.

How well were you received by your audience? Invariably, we see ourselves completely differently to how an audience perceives us - we are either unjustly critical of ourselves, blissfully unaware, or too arrogant to realise we're doing something wrong! Believe it or not, this is completely normal.

Ultimately, it's the audience's response that will determine whether or not you were successful. Sometimes, it can be a little difficult to gauge an audience's response and, unless you speak to each person individually, you can never know for sure, unless they provide some feedback.

Whether commendation or disapproval, feedback offers an audience's objective evaluation of your speech and presentation skills and provides an opportunity for affirmation, reflection, self-improvement, and change.

Ask for feedback *and* give yourself feedback. Being honest with yourself and accepting feedback from others is critical to personal growth - if we cannot accept advice or constructive criticism, we cannot hope to grow. Every speaker who values their craft understands there is always room for improvement. Accomplished speakers embrace feedback, viewing it as an effective learning tool. Their mission is to be better, or the best at their craft, to stand out and be the most honoured and respected in their field.

Remember though, feedback is also subjective, meaning it is only *one* person's opinion - a speaker may appear perfect to one person, yet another will observe areas to develop and hone. Therefore, you must gather and assess the feedback received from *all* parties, rather than isolating one or two individuals' comments. For example, if only one person offers particular feedback, consider it for what it's worth - the impact or effect it had or will have on an audience, the speech, etc. However, if several people make the same comment, it holds more weight, consequently generating more to think about; it might be worth altering the speech or delivery style, or implementing the recommendation if planning to present the speech again.

Do not think of feedback as criticism or disapproval of your speech or delivery. Think of it as a learning tool - it helps to master your public speaking skills. Change your mindset: welcome feedback as an opportunity to grow.

If a number of recommendations are noted, don't try to fix everything at once, as this can seem overwhelming. Look for one or two recommendations and focus on these. Gradually introduce more improvements, until your speech and delivery are polished.

When presenting a speech, the content and speaker should *always* be ethical and inoffensive: if a person or persons find something offensive, heed the advice and adjust the speech or delivery accordingly.

Offering Feedback

On occasion, a fellow speaker will ask you for feedback. When this happens, it is crucial to look for both their strengths and weaknesses. Telling a speaker that they were fabulous and there is nothing they could have done better is a whitewash and benefits no-one, least of all the speaker. Equally, telling a speaker that they were terrible, or listing everything they could improve upon, is unhelpful and hurtful. Offer something useful for the speaker to reflect on: a suggestion to consider applying, to improve themselves the next time they deliver a speech.

An effective method of feedback is to provide a speaker with examples and solutions, enabling them to identify particular points to which you are referring.

A *commendation* is accomplished using the **What, How,** and **Why** method:

- *What* the speaker did well;

- *How* they achieved this; and

- *Why* it was effective.

Example:

A speaker has just concluded his delivery of a speech about the struggling relationship between himself and his brother, who was later diagnosed with terminal cancer. He tells of the emotional rollercoaster they experience, the inevitable loss of a loved one, and the need for forgiveness because, once they're gone, it's too late. The speaker then asks a colleague for some feedback.

What: (commendation) I felt the speech was well-crafted.

How: (demonstration) It had a clearly defined structure – an opening, body, and conclusion.

Why: (explanation) The attention-grabbing opening about losing a loved one made me want to hear more; the body included 3 points - not too much information to be overwhelming to its listener; and the conclusion wrapped things up nicely, referring back to the beginning of the speech, in that 'life's too short.'

In this example, the speaker receiving the commendation knows exactly what he did well, how he did it, and why it worked.

Be sensitive when offering feedback. If there are multiple suggestions, mention only those that are the most important to work on, providing examples and solutions wherever possible. Remember to lead with words such as, "I felt", or "In my opinion" - you are offering your view, not facts.

A *recommendation* is slightly different, accomplished using the **What**, **Why**, and **How** method:

- *What* the speaker can do to improve the speech or its delivery;

- *Why* it will be effective; and

- *How* to achieve it (using demonstration & explanation).

Using the earlier example, here are some recommendations:

What: (recommendation) I felt the body language and modulation of dialogue lacked some of the intended emotion and could be used more effectively.

Why: (explanation) This would enhance the message; the audience will empathise and climb on board, riding the emotional journey with you, as you retell the story.

How: (demonstration) When relating the moment between you and your brother, having just been given the solemn news he was dying, turn to an imaginary person in a hospital bed and show your reaction, the response you felt; include any emotive dialogue you exchanged, such as, "We'll fight this."

In this example, the speaker receiving the recommendation is able to identify the area the listener feels is in need of improvement, what effect it will likely have on the speech and listener, and how it can be achieved.

Be mindful to deliver feedback sensitively. Cold, hard facts can be upsetting to someone, who may already be feeling insecure after their performance. Consider how you would want advice given to you and treat others the same or, perhaps, with even more sensitivity. Try sandwiching suggestions for improvement between areas in which they performed well: tell them a commendation, then an area of improvement, finishing with another commendation. Advice given in this manner will likely leave a speaker feeling grateful and positive about their experience, rather than resentful and hurt.

Receiving Feedback

Feedback comes from an audience in a variety of forms: *nonverbal,* *verbal,* and **written** response. Nonverbal and verbal feedback is dynamic - it is apparent during and immediately following a speech. Therefore, this type of feedback can have a direct impact on a speech in progress. Written feedback is usually received some time after the event, following a request from the speaker or organiser.

Nonverbal Responses

As you deliver your speech, you should be constantly assessing your audience for receptiveness and support, seeking positive nonverbal responses, such as nodding in agreement, smiles and other affirming facial expressions. These actions help to confirm audience interest and engagement with the speaker.

Shaking their head in disagreement, raising eyebrows in disbelief, eye raising or rolling, and other such expressions, are negative audience reactions, which may demand immediate attention and reassessment of content or delivery, on-the-fly. Try responding with an appropriate comment to the audience, such as, "Now, I understand some of you may not agree with me, but ..." or "It sounds unbelievable, doesn't it? But I can assure you ...," going on to explain why they should trust the information you have given them, thereby also giving credence to your words. Acknowledging the audience in this way keeps them interested and more likely to listen to your viewpoint, rather than 'tuning out,' disregarding, or distrusting anything else you have to say.

When an audience applauds, it does so freely. The level of applause is generally a sign of its approval or disapproval – unenthusiastic or reluctant applause is a telling sign and needs no explanation; conversely, when you have an audience on-side, you'll know it! Rapturous applause is exhilarating; a standing ovation ... wow!

Verbal Responses

An audience's laughter, in response to humour or wit, is one of the most wondrous sounds a speaker can experience. Comedians live for it! Speakers love it, too. Laughter relaxes an audience, warms them to the speaker, and makes them more receptive to the speaker's ideas or thoughts. The adage is true:

laughter is the best medicine. But try not to laugh at your own humour or jokes, or at least, not all of them - it comes across as cocky. And, if the audience don't laugh, but you do, it can be rather embarrassing.

Calls of joy, whooping, whistling, hooraying, and other forms of verbal affirmation are invigorating and encouraging - the more the merrier, though preferably at the end of a speech.

Heckling, on the other hand, provides either positive or negative feedback, during a speech. It is better to address a heckler fleetingly, rather than ignoring or focussing too much attention on them, particularly if their behaviour becomes distracting to the speaker or audience.

Positive heckling - people calling out to converse or agree with a speaker - is reassuring but, if distracting, may cause a speaker to lose their train of thought and can annoy an audience. If it happens during your speech, just smile, be humble, perhaps say, "Thank you," or nod, and move on. Enjoy the moment, but don't make a big deal out of it, or you may look conceited; it could be mistaken as a cue for the person to continue heckling and will become bothersome.

Negative heckling can embarrass or shame a speaker and cause them to lose their way … or worse. Try not to let the heckler's comment affect you too deeply. If necessary, address the heckler, without being rude, perhaps saying, "I appreciate your comment. In my experience ..." or "I understand not everyone will agree with me. Evidence shows ...", or use a similar, appropriate response. Keep it factual and succinct. Avoid using the word 'but.' The aim is to maintain credibility whilst avoiding a verbal altercation developing.

However, there will be times when heckling is best ignored.

Written Responses

After an event, the organiser often asks an audience to complete a form or questionnaire, to provide written feedback. The information is then collected and analysed, and any worthwhile feedback used to improve future events. As a speaker, you could do this, too.

Written feedback is just as important to you as a speaker, as it is to an event organiser, as it usually contains far more detail than you would normally receive. It is worthwhile requesting a copy of any feedback from the organiser, or ask for only the feedback pertinent to you.

Alternatively, directly ask the audience for feedback. This can be done at the conclusion of your speech. Some speakers arrange for personalised feedback forms to be distributed and later collected, whilst others provide an email address for people to contact them with feedback, comments, or questions. Feedback forms and emails can provide an opportunity to build a database of prospective clients. However, ensure you have a tick box on the form, or similar, asking whether they wish to be contacted. People won't want to receive unsolicited emails or phone calls, just because they provided feedback – respect their privacy.

CHAPTER 4

Introductions

Make It Count!

"For, usually and fitly, the presence of an introduction is held to imply that there is something of consequence and importance to be introduced."
Arthur Machen

Whether you are introducing a speaker, or you are the speaker being introduced, it must be done correctly. Imagine attending a convention as keynote speaker, only to have your speech topic or credentials cited incorrectly or your name pronounced wrongly. Or perhaps your introduction consists merely of your name and speech topic, nothing else. Would you be concerned? You should be!

Admittedly, it can be upsetting, and perhaps affect your performance; it may even set the tone for poor reception from the audience, who might have expected something different from you. Equally, a few non-substantive words are feeble and pointless. Don't let it happen!

Correctly planned and executed, introductory remarks set the mood for the speaker and speech, create a common bond between speaker and audience, and can mean the difference between a successful event or a failure, so take it seriously. Make it count!

Perhaps the audience know the speaker well, so it doesn't seem to matter as much – they've probably heard it all before? No matter how well an audience knows the speaker, there still needs to be a separation between audience and speaker – an introduction provides this separation. An introduction also provides an opportunity to present the speaker's credentials - authority, knowledge, and experience - on the topic to the listeners, thus adding to his credibility.

As Emcee or speaker, the introduction must be effective!

The Mini-Speech

An introduction is a mini-speech of 15-30 seconds (preferably, no more than one minute), comprised of an opening, body, and conclusion, delivered to prepare the audience to be receptive to the speaker and speech.

An introduction is serious stuff! That said, it doesn't mean you can't be witty, humorous, or fun - though, never use humour to denigrate the speaker, even in fun - it means, every speaker deserves the courtesy of being introduced thoughtfully, respectfully, and correctly, in a manner that is helpful to both speaker and audience.

If an introduction is only 15-30 seconds, how can we possibly create such a short introduction with all the elements of a speech? It's not as hard you think. Let's look at it in detail.

Audiences want to know what's in it for them:

- What is the speech about?

- Why should I listen to this speaker?

- What relevance does the speech have to me?

Introductions can range in complexity, but should always include answers to these three basic questions, in whichever order is suitable for the occasion, for an audience to understand the benefit of listening to the speech.
How the introduction is crafted and delivered is also determined by the occasion, i.e., whether formal or informal.

Formal

Formal introductions are far more important than informal introductions, since an audience doesn't typically get an opportunity to ask the usual questions a person might ask in an informal setting.

A formal introduction includes answers to the three basic questions and is delivered in a formal manner. For example:

"As we struggle through our daily lives and workload, hoping to succeed, taking care of ourselves tends to get forgotten or put on the backburner. Anxiety and stress are frequently a result of this and, often, we're left to our own devices to battle on. Our next speaker has fought his own measure of battles and won, having developed some simple practices to help overcome many dark periods in his life. He now travels the globe, sharing these techniques with emergency responders, pilots, oil rig workers, factory workers, CEO's, and more, with fantastic results. Here to discuss stress and how it impacts us, and to impart some simple wellness techniques we can incorporate in our everyday lives, please welcome our speaker, Mr. ……."

The introduction clearly advises listeners what to expect:

- What is the speech is about – stress & how it affects us.

- Why should I listen – I'll learn about taking care of myself & using wellness techniques to avoid or manage stress.

- What relevance does it have to me – I work in a stressful industry; I am likely to experience stress at some stage.

In this example, the introduction espouses the speaker's credentials: the speaker has personal experience dealing with stress; he used his techniques successfully in combatting stress; and shared the techniques with others, who achieved similar results. While the speaker did not claim professional qualifications relevant to the speech, his life experiences certainly give him a degree of credibility on the topic.

The structure was apparent, too:

- Opening – The importance of self-care to avoid stress.

- Body – How the speaker has suffered stress, overcome stress, and shares wellness techniques to help others.

- Conclusion – How stress affects people; 'Call to Action' to incorporate the techniques in everyday life.

Informal

An informal introduction also includes answers to the three basic questions, but is delivered in a more relaxed way.

For example:

"Boys and girls, we have a special visitor today, who is here to tell you all about his adventures travelling around Egypt. He has a wealth of knowledge, some great stories to tell, and you'll be able to ask him questions about the great pyramids we've been studying. Please put your hands together to welcome, Mr. ...."

The introduction clearly lets students know what to expect:

- What is the speech is about – travelling around Egypt.

- Why should I listen – I will hear some stories and lots of information about Egypt and the pyramids.

- What relevance does it have to me – I am studying Egypt in class; he has stories to tell that relate to my studies; he will be able to answer any questions I may have.

An informal, social introduction, is less specific, but can benefit greatly when more thought is put into it.

Imagine being at a party; you observe your partner talking with another woman. As you approach, your partner turns to you and says, "This is Jo." Nothing else! At this point, all you know is the woman's name, nothing more – such as how long your partner has known her, where they know each other from, the relevance to you, and so forth. It is up to you, now, to find out by asking questions, or remaining oblivious and, perhaps, feeling detached from any further conversation. A better, more informative and interesting introduction would have been, "This is Jo. We went to school together. We were just talking about when she used to help me with my math homework."

Now you have a better idea of who Jo is and her relationship to your partner. The additional knowledge may even relate to previous discussions you have had with your partner regarding her trouble grasping math at school. These simple, extra pieces of information have now created a greater connection to yourself and Jo.

Whilst informal and the briefest of mini-speeches, it is just that, a mini-speech, offering pertinent information to the listener to gauge information of relevance, so they feel more connected and engaged.

Emcee

It is almost certain that you will be called upon, at some time, to introduce someone. The situation may arise in an informal setting, such as introducing a friend to your partner, or a new member of the group. Alternatively, it may occur in a formal gathering, such as a wedding reception, conference, or special event. Whether formal or informal, you are essentially fulfilling the role of an Emcee.

As Emcee, your role is to create and effectively deliver a mini-speech for each person you are expected to introduce - you are preparing the audience to formulate a mindset of receptiveness and respect for the speaker and his message.

An introduction should not be dull and boring, as this could set a negative tone and be reflected in the audience's opinion of a speech. Introductions should be full of enthusiasm and energy to 'prime' the audience – revving them up, getting people excited about what they're about to hear – so they'll want to stay and listen, rather than be distracted texting on their phones, or leave to get a coffee.

Enticing an audience with some rhetorical questions or 'what if' scenarios, relative to the topic to be presented, adds thought-provoking and exciting elements to an introduction.

If you know and like the speaker, include positive recognition in your opening – if the audience know and like you, they will trust you and are more likely to feel positive about the speaker, too.

Introductions can be entertaining, too, so don't be afraid to include wit and humour. Make it fun. However, all attention should be directed toward the speaker - the idea is to compliment him, not steal the show!

Be mindful of the event when planning an introduction – it will usually dictate what is suitable. For example, a humorous or witty introduction at a solemn occasion would be inappropriate, of course.

Let's imagine you are the Emcee assigned to introduce a speaker. Firstly, you must confirm the speaker's name and credentials:

- Determine the correct pronunciation of the speaker's name.

  Tip: If possible, converse with the speaker personally, rather than receiving second or third-hand information. Write the name down phonetically, if required, so you will remember the pronunciation when you have to say it again later. Do not guess or assume it's the same as previously heard – this may cause embarrassment.

- Obtain important and relevant credential information about the speaker.

  Tip: Wherever possible, converse with the speaker in

advance, such as by phone, email, or in-person, to ensure the information is relevant, current, and accurate.

- Obtain the speech subject or topic, the reason for presenting to this audience, and why at this time.

    Tip: This makes up the *body* of the introduction, which covers the audience's "What's in it for me?" questions.

Secondly, prepare an effective introduction incorporating the information you've gathered:

- **Opening** – Grab the audience's attention, alerting them to the importance of the subject and the speaker's relevant expertise.

    Tip: Your audience needs to believe the speaker is worthy of their attention. Pique the audience's interest or curiosity, without giving away too much of the speech.

- **Body** – Set the mood of the audience for the speech to come; it briefly explains what the topic is about, why the audience should listen, and what relevance it has to the listener.

    Tip: Be careful not to give too much of the speech away. Build audience expectation, alluding to the topic, without removing the speaker's impact. Only say what needs to be said to arouse their curiosity and interest.

- **Conclusion** – Summarise what the speech is about; lead with an inspiring or exciting line, if suitable; and finish with an audience applause-inducing sentence, stating the speaker's name so the audience can relate the name to the topic: " ... Here to discuss stress and how it impacts us, and to impart some simple wellness techniques we can incorporate in our everyday lives, please welcome our speaker, Mr. ...."

  Tip: Welcome the speaker to the stage, by leading the applause; walk toward the speaker as they approach and acknowledge them, shaking hands (if usual protocol dictates) then leave the stage/sit down. As Emcee, you should remain on stage until it is handed over to the next speaker; alternatively, gesture with an open-palmed hand toward the speaker and as they walk on stage, you leave in the opposite direction.

Finally, once the speaker has concluded their speech:

- Lead the applause, whilst approaching the stage briskly, to avoid leaving the stage empty. Remember to shake hands with the speaker, if such protocol was followed earlier. Continue to lead the applause until the speaker has left the stage, perhaps turning your body in the direction toward the departing speaker, for emphasis.

- Acknowledge the speaker with a few words of thanks on behalf of the audience; you may briefly compliment the speaker and/or speech, if appropriate.

  Tip: Be succinct. Only make comments that relate to the speaker's intention or purpose. Do not give your personal opinion of the speech.

Once you have prepared the introduction, you should edit, rehearse, and deliver it in the same manner you would any speech, making sure each introduction does not exceed 30-60 seconds.

Transition

An Emcee should be able to provide an appropriate transition between multiple speakers, helping connect speakers, topics, or ideas, which might otherwise seem vague and obscure.

When transitioning between speakers, it is an Emcee's responsibility to prepare audiences for mood or tone changes, too, particularly when the topics differ considerably: a humorous speech on Millennial kids, followed by a sensitive speech on the increased death rate of prostate cancer victims, needs to be handled differently; the transitional introduction helps change the atmosphere in the room, ready for the next speaker.

Ensure you have access to the agenda or running sheet for the event, showing the order of speaking, topics, and so forth, and prepare each transitional introduction accordingly.

Be prepared for changes in the order of speaking, which can occur at the last minute – right up until the moment a speaker is due on stage!

Your Introduction

Being formally introduced at an event is exciting; it is also an honour and privilege, and should not be taken lightly. Brushing off your introduction as being unimportant is a mistake neither you nor the Emcee want to make.

There are several wrong ways to be introduced, which can affect an audience's first impression of you. These are:

- Hopeful – "I'm sure he'll be great."

- DIY – "His bio speaks for itself."

- Regurgitation – "As his bio says ..."

- Adulation – "This speaker needs no introduction."

None of these introductions are helpful, in any way; they are a lazy way of introducing a speaker.

You will want the Emcee to prepare the audience to receive your speech appropriately, presenting the correct and most relevant information, as well as note proper pronunciation of your name and qualifications. A well organised Emcee will ask for your biography (bio) before the event, to prepare an effective introduction. However, if you are not contacted for information and the event is only days away, contact the Emcee or organiser. Don't leave it till the last minute, if you can help it. Provide a brief (15-30 second) bio of yourself, along with the topic and synopsis of the speech, without giving away too much – effectively, you will have more control over what is said: your relevant credentials are outlined and the crux of your speech is not revealed too early.

Ask the Emcee to forward a copy of the introduction to you, once completed, so any errors, omissions, or changes can be made before the event. Don't forget to thank the Emcee for working with you to create a great introduction.

It is quite common for a speaker to write or outline his own introduction, especially if there is particular information he wishes to convey. Providing an Emcee with a well-scripted intro is accepted practice, as it prevents incorrect or irrelevant information being relayed to the audience and ad-libbing or over-zealous Emcees producing a verbal juggling act, perhaps destroying your credibility. It is also very useful if there is any uncertainty as to the capability of the Emcee formulating an effective introduction. Your reputation is on the line, so you want it done right!

However, when providing a pre-scripted intro, be gracious in allowing the Emcee freedom of expression to alter (or shorten, if time-critical) the introduction, as he sees fit. Still ask for a copy or discuss any changes to reach a mutually agreeable solution.

CHAPTER 5

Tips For Success

Do's & Don'ts

"Believe in your ideas and be the best."
Richard Branson

To be a better speaker, i.e., to improve our speech writing and public speaking ability and technique, we need to know our strengths and weaknesses: what we're doing right, what we can do better, and what to avoid. In this chapter, we'll focus on preparation and delivery techniques.

Remember, one of our greatest tools is a smartphone or video camera. Using a smartphone or video camera to record your rehearsals then review them, will help identify any issues with the speech - you can edit or rewrite as necessary - as well as work on improving your delivery strengths and eliminating any weaknesses before delivering the speech to an audience. With self-reflection and persistence, you will become a better speaker.

There are countless do's and don'ts, actions that, whilst preparing or delivering a speech, can have profound effects on both speaker and audience. It is impossible to list them all – this book would be too large to print!

Although already addressed in earlier chapters, and to reinforce their importance, I've included some main, preferred actions a speaker should aim to incorporate in his delivery, to help illustrate how each action is accomplished and explain its effect on an audience.

Later in this chapter, I've revealed several common mistakes speakers make, or weaknesses they display, and provided some tips on how to avoid them.

Strive to Succeed

Audience: Identify your audience and prepare a suitable speech; be mindful of cultural diversity, as well as the language and terminology used. The speaker is audience-centric; it shows respect and understanding of the audience.

Speech Style: Choose a speech style befitting the audience, topic, message, and environment. The speaker is audience-centric; it shows respect and appropriateness for listeners and the occasion.

Know When Enough is Enough: Be succinct; tailor your speech to include only the vital points necessary to achieve the desired result; define the message and identify two or three key points to accomplish this. Using supporting facts, material, anecdotes, etc., to convey your message effectively keeps the audience on-topic, focussed, and engaged.

Venue: Check out the venue beforehand to get a feel for the space. If impractical, arrive early and confirm everything is in order before the audience arrives; this helps familiarise and settle the speaker to prepare for effective delivery, to avoid any potential problems occurring.

Approach: Walk confidently and calmly to your speaking position; this conveys confidence in oneself and the topic.

Posture: Stand up straight, erect; this conveys confidence.

Body Language & Hand Gestures: Practise well and use body language & hand gestures appropriately; include wherever it looks and feels natural; this enhances a speech and is more engaging to the audience.

Eye contact: Maintain regular eye contact; hold your focus longer on individuals at important or poignant moments of speech; this helps to connect and engage an audience.

Vocal Variety: Use modulation, emphasis, pace, and pause to effect; use a pause to gather your thoughts or between sentences; this adds colour and meaning to the information; entertains; engages and connects; enables the audience to absorb content; and avoids the use of annoying filler words.

Notes: Speak without notes, whenever possible; this conveys subject knowledge and credibility and improves audience receptiveness and confidence in the speaker.

Stage Movement: Position yourself at various points on the stage while you deliver the speech, particularly if it is a large stage; move only with purpose; alter your stage position when transitioning between main points. The audience will feel more connected and their attention will be drawn toward you; the audience can identify when each main point concludes and you are moving onto the next.

Audience Interaction: Incorporate effective interaction and participation, such as physical involvement or rhetorical questions; this keeps the audience engaged, interested, and entertained.

Aids & Props: Use eye-catching or practical aids and props to demonstrate or explain; it enhances a speech and changes the audience's focus, keeping them alert and attentive.

Experience: Accept public speaking opportunities whenever possible, to practise your craft and gain valuable experience; ensure you are well-prepared before each event. Practising skills learned will hasten your public speaking journey and help build confidence.

Prevent Mistakes

"A person who never made a mistake, never tried anything new."
Albert Einstein

Making mistakes is inevitable – we *all* make them occasionally. Minor slip-ups or stumbles are to be expected; it's not the end of the world. How frequently mistakes occur can be reduced by proper preparation; taking responsibility for those errors and preventing recurrences will lead to success.

As every doctor can attest, 'Prevention is better than cure.' Public speaking is the same principle: minimising the chance of problems occurring is the way to go. Here are some examples of mistakes, demonstrating cause and effect, and useful tips on how to avoid them:

Audience: Having a 'one-speech-fits-all' mentality appears disrespectful and shows a lack of understanding of the audience and its needs.

Tip: Tailoring the topic, language, terminology, and message for each audience will ensure understanding and engagement; this is an audience-centric approach.

Information Overload: Including too many main points and sub-points, or details, facts & figures, and a vague, or unclear message confuses and disengages the audience and leaves a speaker with little, or no, credibility.

Tip: Ensure the topic suits the audience; be succinct; limit the points and details to those necessary to convey your message and interest listeners, without overwhelming them.

Opening Line: Opening with "My name is ...", or "My speech is about . . .", or "... I hope you enjoy my speech", or use filler words (ah's, um's, etc.), to begin a speech conveys lack of confidence, professionalism, and preparedness.

Tip: Discuss your introduction with the Emcee before the speech to ensure both speaker and topic are properly introduced. Remember, your opening should already have been prepared to provide an understanding of the topic and generate impact, inviting the audience on a journey with you.

Speech Style: Using incorrect or inappropriate speech style, such as a casual style in a formal or corporate environment, will appear inappropriate and disrespectful, and will likely disengage an audience, or perhaps open a speaker to constant interruption during delivery.

Tip: Learn as much as you can about the audience and the setting; perhaps confirm the chosen speech style with the organiser to prevent embarrassment or misunderstanding.

Venue: Failing to inspect or inquire of the venue, such as when needing a projector for slides, or microphone/audio equipment will appear ill-prepared and inexperienced.

Tip: Ask about the venue and setting; discuss any technical or audio equipment requirements with organisers, such as electrical power points, leads, converters, microphones, speakers, etc. This helps to be prepared, prevent embarrassment, and appear professional. Arrive early and check out the venue to confirm everything is in order before the audience arrives.

Stage Fright: Being afraid, hesitating, unable to enter the stage, tongue-tied, or dumbstruck – these actions all convey fear, unpreparedness, and a lack of confidence.

Tip: Before entering the stage practise the relaxation techniques that you found were most effective for you; if already on stage, subtly practise diaphragmatic breathing – helps settle nerves and relieve anxiety & tension (refer to Chapter 2).

Confidence: Overtly displaying fear or a lack of confidence; copying or mimicking another speaker; these actions cause embarrassment to the speaker, unsettle the audience, and appear false and phony, resulting in a loss of credibility for the speaker.

Tip: Focus on the topic, not your performance; after all, you know your stuff and the audience want to listen to you – it wants you to succeed. Be yourself! Don't try to be someone you're not - be natural, do your best, and your confidence will improve with practice and further experience.

Approach: Hurrying on or off stage can be interpreted in several ways, from fear and insecurity to arrogance, and can be irritating to an audience.

Tip: Be confident, without appearing conceited; approach the stage calmly and take up your position; leave the stage in the same manner; before going on stage practise the relaxation techniques to release anxiety and tension (refer to Chapter 2).

Posture: Slouching shoulders, appearing hunched over, or with your head down conveys a lack of confidence, fear, and uncertainty.

Tip: Stand up straight, erect; look and feel self-assured and believe in yourself; this will radiate to your audience and help improve credibility.

Body Language: Using inappropriate body language or behaviour - repetitive movements, or actions that are over the top and overacted - appears unnatural, awkward, and staged. This lacks authenticity and can be irritating.

Tip: Use suitable body language that complements and enhances a speech, and looks and feels natural; ensure any actions or movements do not offend an audience.

Hand Gestures: Using inappropriate or incongruent gestures, or repetitive motions appears unnatural, distracting, and annoying.

Tip: Use hand gestures to complement and enhance a speech, and which look and feel natural; ensure any gestures do not cause offence to an audience.

Eye contact: Looking up at the ceiling or down at the floor, or eyes flitting back and forth 'hosing' the audience exudes insecurity or forgotten speech and is likely to disconnect or disengage the audience.

Tip: It can feel uncomfortable, even disconcerting, looking directly at the audience whilst speaking or gathering your thoughts, especially while you are inexperienced. An effective, albeit temporary, solution to use is to focus on an area just above the listener's head, giving the appearance you are looking directly at them, even though you're not. With practice and experience, you will eventually become comfortable looking directly at an audience.

Vocal Variety: Speaking ineffectually - in a hurried or rushed pace; without using pauses; in monotone, i.e., in the same tone with no inflection or emphasis; and overusing filler words – demonstrates a speaker's, unpreparedness, and lack of confidence, credibility, and conviction. This will bore, annoy, or irritate an audience – listeners may even decide to leave!

Tip: Practise different delivery techniques, such as adding tone, inflection, light & shade, and pause - for dramatic effect - to create a more engaging speech. Pause between sentences and when thinking to yourself to allow an audience time to absorb the information while you gather your thoughts.

Notes: Using excessive notes, reading a speech verbatim, or shuffling papers, demonstrates a lack of subject knowledge, experience, and confidence; it restricts movement, hand gestures, and body language, and can irritate an audience.

Tip: Use small cards to prevent papers rustling (if kept on the lectern you can use very thick paper) with the speech outline written as brief notes or bullet points to help jog your memory. Only refer to them when necessary - do not rely on them like a 'crutch.'.

Stage Movement: Standing stock-still; shuffling your feet; clicking the heels of your shoes on the floor; and aimless wandering – these are pointless actions that can appear stilted & cold, or irritating & frustrating to an audience.

Tip: If circumstances limit movement, use body language & hand gestures effectively to help compensate and relieve stiffness, creating a more animated delivery; be aware of footwear and movement and the effect it has on different floor surfaces; move with purpose to enhance the speech and audience connectedness.

Fidgeting, Tics, & Other Annoying Actions: Fiddling with your clothes; unconscious clapping; hands clasped or in prayer; hands on hips; hands in pockets; arms folded or behind your back; using irritating and repetitive actions; thigh or leg slapping; resting on one heel or toe pointing; foot-stomping; sniffing; wiping your nose with your hand or on your sleeve; slurping from a glass or drink bottle; having an unkempt appearance, etc. These and more – it's a seemingly endless list of actions – create aggravation, annoyance, and distraction, disengaging the audience, causing the speaker to lose credibility and the audience's respect.

Tip: Use a smartphone or video to record your delivery and identify any actions that might aggravate or irritate an audience; we are usually blissfully unaware we are performing any of these actions until we see them on video! Rehearse regularly, eliminating one action at a time. Do not overwhelm yourself by trying to perfect everything at once, as you'll likely take one step forward and two steps back. Take one step at a time - baby steps - and you will improve with practice.

Procrastination: Putting off planning, preparing, rehearsing, or anything else! Stalling or delaying the inevitable is foolish and leads to disaster - a speaker appears unprepared, discourteous, and unprofessional, and will not be asked to return.

Tip: Don't procrastinate! Give yourself the best chance to succeed - start out early, to be as ready as you can be.

Closing: concluding the speech with counterproductive content or comments such as:

- Introducing new information or material – the sudden inclusion of new information causes audience confusion;

- "In conclusion," "Finally," or "I'll close with" – causes and audience to 'switch off' and stop listening;

- "Are there any questions?" – followed by an awkward silence, can leave an impression of a disinterested audience, especially if no questions are forthcoming.

Tip: Most importantly, *never* introduce new information to the audience during the conclusion (closing); the conclusion is used to summarise the speech and provide closure; presenting new information defeats this purpose and will confuse listeners. An effective closing briefly summarises the main points, referring them back to the central idea; it restates the through-line, tying everything together, thereby reminding the audience of the message, and leaving them able to apply it to their own lives. It may also include a 'Call to Action.' Delivered in this manner, it will be obvious to an audience the speech has concluded.

If you will be including a Q&A segment following the speech, offering to 'open the floor for questions' is a good technique. However, have a prepared question and answer ready, should there be no questions from the audience. If time is limited, don't be afraid to say it: "I'm almost out of time, but I can take one quick question, or I'll be happy to take any questions at the end of the evening." Using this terminology, any awkward silence will not be noticeable, as an audience will expect you to wrap up quickly, respecting that you are time-critical, and will likely save their question for later.

Apologizing: Offering apologies for lateness, mistakes, or being ill-prepared – the audience will become off-side and disengaged; the speaker will lose credibility.

Tip: Never draw needless attention to things the audience probably did not notice anyway. Aim to arrive early and be adequately prepared; in unseen circumstances, have the Emcee's contact details on hand, and let them know what is happening; a good Emcee will entertain an audience to avoid the speaker's embarrassment. Audience members want you to succeed, as they've given their valuable time to come and listen to you – regardless of how you feel inside, present yourself confidently, but without appearing arrogant.

Gratitude, & Hopefulness: Saying "Thank you for coming," "I hope you like my speech," or "I trust you learned something, from my speech," and so forth – 'hopeful' and 'grateful' remarks present as insecurity, inexperience, or even conceit.

Tip: Comments should be affirming, not denigrating; avoid thanking the audience at the outset – people have come to hear you speak and should be thanking *you*, not the reverse. If you feel compelled to thank them, do so after the speech, simply saying, "Thank you." If you doubt or belittle yourself, why would people want to listen to you, or believe you? On the other hand, over-confidence can appear arrogant or patronising. Have faith in yourself and be guided by the audience reaction: smiles, nods in agreement, applause, and other feedback are true indications of an effective speech - you don't have to state the fact!

Experience: Shying away from, hesitating, or rejecting opportunities to practise public speaking – failure to accept might result in not being offered another opportunity!

Tip: Organisers may only ask once, for fear of rejection, so accept any suitable offers to speak publicly. As the adage says, 'Practice makes perfect' – the more you practice your craft, the more relaxed you will become, thereby building your confidence. You will learn from each experience and using the feedback you receive to help perfect your craft.

Self-Doubt: Never beginning, for fear of failure – this is counterproductive, detrimental, and just plain wrong!

Tip: Believe it's possible. As my father always said to me, "You can do anything you put your mind to." So wise!

~

You have now read through this book; practised some simple techniques to manage the fear; learned how to create, develop, and deliver an audience-centred speech; and probably completed the first of many speeches to come. You delivered a speech and, whilst it may have felt like the world was ending, you survived. Congratulations! As I said in Chapter 1, you won't die. And guess what? You didn't!

Now, you might be thinking it's all over, but this is only the beginning. Who knows when the next public speaking opportunity will be? Perhaps you'll use the skills acquired at your next job interview, a friend's wedding, a work presentation; or when delivering a eulogy. Take what you've learnt, and the feedback you've received, to improve yourself and become a better speaker, so that when the time comes and whatever the occasion, you will be the best that you can be.

Author's Note

It is always a thrill and sense of accomplishment when we finish something; for me, it is writing this book. I'm sure you, too, will be feeling a sense of achievement, having worked your way through the book. Congratulations on the courage and commitment you've shown to your public speaking journey. We all had to begin somewhere, and I am grateful to have shared the journey with you.

This, by no means, is all there is to know about public speaking – it would require a lot more detail and result in a much larger book. But it is a start and is aimed at helping readers commence their journey, without finding it too daunting to take that first step.

Finding time to set aside to write a speech can be a challenge in itself; I had the same difficulty while writing this book. But it is a must if we plan to succeed. Being in the right headspace and environment is important, too, with many a cool winter afternoon, or warm summer day, spent sitting in the alfresco, blissfully tapping away at my laptop keyboard, and only the sweet sound of bird calls, or trees rustling in the breeze, to accompany me; with perhaps an occasional neighbour's mower to puncture my peace.

This book was partly inspired by my own experiences and my father's inspirational quote, but mostly from a life-long commitment to helping people. Finally putting pen to paper – well actually, 'fingers on a keyboard' – has been a wonderful exercise and life experience for me as an author, and realising the book's potential for a positive effect on you, its reader. And whether it helps one million readers or just one reader, it will have achieved its purpose.

Please feel free to contact me anytime on my website: premierpublicspeaking.com - I would love to hear of your success stories, or not-so-successful stories and what you learned from them.

Wishing you all the best on your public speaking journey.

References

1 Martin Joos, *The Five Clocks*. Bloomington: Indiana University Research Center in Anthropology, Folklore, and Linguistics.

2 World Health Organization 2009, *Distribution of suicides rates (per 100 000) by gender and age*, 2000, World Health Organization, Geneva 27, Switzerland.

Notes